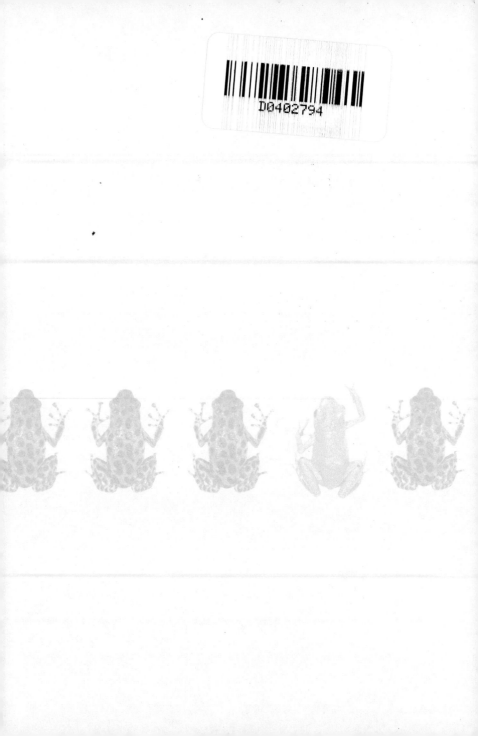

D0402794

THE ONE WHO IS NOT BUSY

THE ONE WHO IS NOT BUSY

Connecting with Work in
a Deeply Satisfying Way

DARLENE COHEN

Gibbs Smith, Publisher
Salt Lake City

First Edition

08   07   06   05   04   5   4   3   2

Text © 2004 Darlene Cohen

Published by
Gibbs Smith, Publisher
P.O. Box 667
Layton, Utah 84041

1.800.748.5439 orders
www.gibbs-smith.com

Designed and produced by Kathleen Szawiola
Printed and bound in the U.S.A.

Library of Congress Cataloging-in-Publication Data
Cohen, Darlene.
   The one who is not busy : connecting with work in a deeply satisfying
way / Darlene Cohen.— 1st ed.
      p. cm.
   Includes bibliographical references.
   ISBN 1-58685-251-5
   1. Job satisfaction. 2. Quality of work life. 3. Time management.
   4. Organizational effectiveness. 5. Attention. I. Title.
HF5549.5.J63 C63 2004
650.1—dc22

                                             2003024950

ACKNOWLEDGMENTS

Basically Gibbs Smith (known variously as Gibbs-dogg or G-doggy-dog) is responsible for the writing of this book. He came to Tassajara to attend a workshop on time and activity called "The One Who Is Not Busy," based on the 21st case in *The Book of Serenity,* a collection of Zen *koans.* His combination of intellectual curiosity and big, wide-open heart inspired me enormously in my teaching there. I treasure his enthusiasm for the "One Who Is Not Busy" and his compassion for the busy ones.

I will always be grateful to my teachers: Michael Wenger, Blanche Hartman, Richard Baker, Meir Schneider, and a sizable slice of suffering humanity, some of whose stories are in this book.

I would like to thank my dear husband, the very good-looking Tony Patchell, who is the Genuine One in our family. He has inspired and sustained me for years.

I also thank Johanna Buchert Smith for her sharp editing

abilities. I am the kind of writer whose intelligibility hangs on an editor's attention to detail.

I wrote most of this book while sequestered for that purpose at the Spokane home of my dear friend, Daya Goldschlag. She brought tea and a bagel with homemade jam to my computer desk every morning, and her insights into the churned-out pages to my lawn chair every afternoon. She also built gourmet meals and swimming trips to lakes into my writing schedule so that I, too, could be the busy and not busy one.

I agreed to write this book when I met Gibbs Smith during a five-day workshop on the topic of time and busyness at Tassajara Hot Springs, a Zen Buddhist retreat center in Big Sur. I co-facilitated the workshop "The One Who Is Not Busy" with Basya Petnick and Rabbi Helen Cohn. Gibbs was quite taken with the notion of "simultaneous inclusion," that a worker could be both "busy" and "not busy" at the same time. "Is that enlightenment?" he asked me once after a delicious breakfast prepared by the monks at Tassajara and eaten in a charmingly rustic dining room. "Gibbs," I replied, blissfully stuffed with buckwheat pancakes and maple syrup, "if you've got simultaneous inclusion, you don't need enlightenment."

We agreed "The One Who Is Not Busy" would make a great book on a happening, business-world topic. Despite my overflowing schedule of clients and teaching, I took on the writing of this book because I am very animated by the topic and thought it would be quick and easy to write. Gibbs only wanted a small book setting out the basics of the workshop, which I had been teaching around the country for nearly a year. I also prided myself on my personal mastery of the art of busyness itself. Because of the very skills I was teaching, I could add one more thing to my list of projects that I wanted to do.

Once the book was contracted, setting a deadline only three months away, I realized I should have been writing all along. Basically, I was too busy to write this book! My solution was to append an extra day or two onto a couple of weekends and try to finish the book in four three- and four-day patches. The problem is, though, if I go too long without unstructured time—a whole day off with nothing to do—I get grumpy and tired. I can't concentrate any longer. In order to emerge whole from the demanding schedule I was setting for writing this book, working straight through four weekends, I would have to practice what I'm about to preach to you—I would have to totally submerge myself in "not busy" while madly and busily working away.

You hold in your hands the proof that this approach works. I fervently practiced *Skill 1: The ability to narrow or widen the mind's focus at will,* and *Skill 2: The mental flexibility to shift the mind's focus at will from one thing to another (to go from "narrow"* to *"narrow"* to *"narrow"*), as if to save my head from fire. My computer sits in front of a wall of windowpanes, allowing me to look out at the redwood grove in which my house is situated. I diligently typed away in two-hour stretches, organizing and expressing my thoughts about busyness. Every once in a while, as I was thinking over the context and clarity of what I had just written, I raised my eyes to the sight of the sun dappling through the trees outside my window, right over my computer's screen. Thus, *Skill 1* provided the widening of context, which kept me energized and focused for hours at a time.

Since I was writing over a period of days, life intruded with its characteristic relentlessness. I had to pay bills, cook meals, pick up mail at the post office, return phone calls, maintain conjugal bliss. Employing *Skill 2,* I shifted my full attention to each activity in turn. Thus, each task greatly refreshed me. I totally immersed myself in writing this book while I was at the computer. Whenever I left my desk to do other chores, I totally immersed myself in the new activity as well. Walking to the post office, I enjoyed the woodsy fragrance, the beautiful colors of summer flowers, and the doings of my neighbors along the way. I didn't give the book a single thought on these jaunts. (I'm a great believer in the unconscious workings of the creative process. I totally trust my subconscious mind to work on a project while I am refreshing myself.) Despite a panic or two in which I was terrified I wouldn't be able to finish by the deadline, I continually practiced bringing my focus back to the task at hand, the one under my nose. Panic is caused by projection onto the future and is readily allayed by attention to the present.

From listening to people who take my classes and workshops on "The One Who Is Not Busy," I have come to understand that I'm not alone in my greed—my inclination to take on too many responsibilities. I call this "greed" because my inclination has a covetous, grasping tenor to it. When I process a request, I first think, quite reasonably, "I can't do this because I already have so many other obligations," but my next thought is, "I can't bear to miss something exciting!" Or "I can't bear to miss something with such promise for the future," or "I can't bear to miss this opportunity for working with someone I want to know better," or "I can't pass up something that will bring me such prestige." I'm not the only one who thinks this; *everybody* takes on more than they have time to do. Nor am I the only one who panics; *everyone* realizes there's not going to be enough time. However, I'm also not the only one who has found it well worth the effort to develop skills that settle the mind.

In the business world it is very consequential to manage time well and to be able to make good decisions on the fly. The way we prioritize tasks, the way we treat our coworkers and employees, the way we respond to a crisis situation, all determine our efficiency and effectiveness. Each of these essential work skills has as its foundation the way we focus our attention. What basically determines our success in the workplace is whether the object of our focus is the most efficacious for the situation, and also how firmly we can maintain the appropriate focus in the face of a constant stream of energy-dissipating distractions, or even how deftly we can integrate the so-called "distractions" into that focal point. Plus, heaps of research has highlighted another factor as fundamental to a business person's ability to bring her full range of creativity and talent to the work tasks before her: the amount of work satisfaction experienced in the day-to-day job life.

It's not wading through another boring week for the pay envelope that makes us resourceful employees and expansive employers. It's not even the euphoric victory at the wrap-up of a long and difficult case or sales campaign. Of course, the triumphant moment of acknowledging a job well done is a significant reward for our labor, but even more motivating is our moment-to-moment work satisfaction, the sense of flow found in the events of each task: errors caught before the report went to the boss; each trip down the corridor to the Xerox room; each shipping order checked and approved; each chuckle shared over another absurd situation. Real satisfaction comes when, instead of forever straining toward the vaunted future when we will be rich, successful, or at least appreciated and a little more secure, we learn to cultivate and recognize the pleasure in every event and encounter in our work life, in every difficulty and challenge.

Over the years that I have been working with people faced with a variety of emotional and professional crises, I have come to believe that one of life's most essential skills is the ability to focus one's attention at will. This single ability is the foundation of all mastery and contentment. We can't talk about developing talent or mining resources until this skill is in place. Mastery over one's attention determines the quality of one's life.

As Mihaly Csikszentmihalyi points out in the "Work" section of his excellent book *Flow: The Psychology of Optimal Experience,* "Any small gain in the realm of conscious experience will make work richer, more enjoyable, more meaningful . . . . Those who take the trouble to gain mastery over what happens in consciousness do live a happier life."[1]

Do we have to take time out to become Zen masters in order to exert control over our conscious attention, or can we develop this as we perform our job in our everyday workplace? The advantage a Zen master has is that he brings a well-regulated consciousness to the task. But we, too, can build on observations and skills we may not yet be aware of. Most of us are already familiar with other people's attention patterns, the specific ways others habitually focus their attention. For instance, a good financial planner truly loves manipulating numbers and devises new ways to relate them to each other for the sheer pleasure of it. He would follow their fluctuations during the day whether his job depended on it or not. A good personnel director intuits from just a few interviews in what way a new hiree may best contribute to the company's welfare and with whom he or she might best start working. A woman who starts her own crafts business must attend to manufacture, distribution, and customer relations; she has to do everything! She'll be successful to the extent that she genuinely enjoys following her products from creation to customers' hands and then doing the books in her spare time to determine the profitability of her efforts.

At an office party, the eager salesman will network for potential customers; the headhunter will notice talent; the marriage-minded temp will scan the crowd for attractive members of the opposite sex; the unfocused, eternally distracted employee will eat and drink enough to produce a pleasant buzz, then mine his nearest companions for appreciation of his own contributions to the conversation. Each of these workers process different relevant signals that others will not notice.

We create ourselves by how we invest our attention. Thus, learning skills to focus and sustain our attention at will is the most significant endeavor we can make in the task of improving the quality of our work lives.

Practicing the skills and exercises set forth in this little book has proven very useful to a wide range of people for getting things done and enjoying both the time spent and the effort exerted along the way. Feel free to relax and enjoy the training itself with its little epiphanies. It will begin immediately to enrich your understanding of reality because the training literally expands your consciousness. If you find that any chores in your life are flat and tiresome, you will be delighted to discover the layers of consciousness that await you in even the most repetitious activities.

Through routine tasks you will not only learn to actually "live," but you will discover that you have the option of examining your own dormant layers of creativity and proficiency with the possibility of expanding your serviceable talents as well.

—*Darlene Cohen*

CHAPTER ONE

The Ones Who Are Busy

■ NANCY

After talking to her client for the third time that afternoon,
Nancy threw the phone down onto the pile of papers covering
the desk of her home office. She pressed her tired back muscles
against her ergonomic chair, retrieved the phone and dialed.
She reached her husband on his cell phone immediately.

"I'm canceling our reservations for the weekend," she told
him, her voice strangled with suppressed emotion. "I have to
prepare another paper for the Tyler case."

"Oh, honey!" But his sympathy was tempered with his own
disappointment. "You've done this to us too often. Don't I matter
as much as your clients do?"

"Not you too!" It was there inside her, and she let it rip.
"Don't you understand that I'm as disappointed as you are?
That I need a break too? How can you add to my burden by
blaming me! Well, I've had it! I need to get away from ALL of

you!" She slammed down the phone and spent the next few minutes with her head on her desk, crying. Finally she lifted her head, wiped her eyes, breathed deeply and dialed her husband's number. Of course she needed to apologize. And his rhetorical question about mattering to her as much as her clients needed to be addressed. By her, by him, by their whole life together. Here she was, doing freelance brief writing at home after quitting an unbearably high-pressure caseload in a large law firm only two years ago, and now she had allowed the number of clients she serviced to climb until she was inundated. It looked like she had to redefine her work once again: not full-time lawyer, not freelance brief writer. She kept needing to parse her job description into ever-smaller units of tasks. Apparently she had no internal means of controlling her workload.

■ LUANN

LuAnn had been a graphic artist before the kids came, and now that her second son was in preschool, she had returned to work part-time in her old firm. She was very anxious to go back to work; she was afraid that her mind was turning to mush. What she hadn't foreseen was that the few hours her kids were gone were not exactly equivalent to unspoken-for time. Packing lunches, driving the kids to school and taking her turn to provide snacks there ate up most of the work hours she'd counted on. Although she saw the problem right away, she tried to do it all anyway. So three months into four-hour workdays and full-time mothering and housekeeping, she knew something had to give, but she couldn't bring herself to quit her job, her outpost of sanity. She slowly came to the anguished realization that everything in her life—being with her kids, planning meals, even making love to her husband—was a chore.

■ **KEN**

Ken is young, talented and energetic. He works for a small, cutting-edge tech firm that develops robotics for toys and home use. The days of taking sleeping bags to work are over, but Ken puts in the hours. His job entails generating a constant stream of original ideas, working out their practical application, and then presenting the ongoing project to company brass. He actually loves the challenge of his work, calls his job "play," bears up under the pressure of the presentations, and is either ecstatic or dejected after his bosses have had their say. The trouble is, he's starting to have the common somatic indications of living under persistent high stress: frequent colds, headaches and muscle spasms in his lower back. Because his job demands all his resourcefulness, his relationship with his girlfriend has

become stagnant. He's usually too tired to give her the attention she would like, so they tend to hang out at home or watch
a video when they're together. No, he'd rather *not* "discuss"
their relationship.

■ MICHAEL

Michael, the owner of his own successful high-end shoe
business in the hip Mission District in San Francisco, began a
meditation practice after an acrimonious divorce led him to
believe he was unaware of much of his motivation in interpersonal affairs. He wanted to find out more about "what makes
me tick." A bonus was that he found meditation practice
extremely relaxing, since he was able to put aside his everyday
cares and focus his mind on his breath. After just a few months
of regular practice, he realized that outside of his regular meditation period, he was rarely relaxed. Although he claims to
enjoy his daily work of creating shoe designs that will later be
manufactured, and supervising the employees of his company,
he admits that his morning meditation state of mind disappears
at the first glimpse of his desk. He can't go from a leisurely
morning cup of tea to arriving at his desk ready to work. He
needs first to rev himself up into "work mode," a state of height-
ened urgency and nervous tension, which he considers a neces-

sary state of mind to keep up while flinging himself at his tasks. There is nothing relaxed or natural about his effort. At the end of the day, he lets go of his near-hysterical mental state and collapses, barely able to interact with his children at dinner, let alone enjoy the nightlife he had intended to put into place after his divorce.

■ RICHARD

At thirty-three years of age, Richard is a relatively young man to be a national accounts manager in the home office of a high-tech communications firm. He had just gotten a much-anticipated promotion less than six months before I met him in the hospital Stress Reduction Program. Working in sales had been, by definition, frenetically paced, but as accounts manager, he was bombarded by a constant stream of multiple inputs from varied sources inside and outside the company. One morning he had to take his children to school because his wife had an early meeting at her own firm. When he got to work an hour later at 9 A.M., he already had more than one hundred e-mails, fifty of which required a definite response ranging from a quick "Yeah, I'll be at the meeting" to answers about several multi-month projects he had to deal with. On top of that, he had fifteen phone calls marked "URGENT," one of them from one of his firm's corporate banking clients that involved an enormous amount of work with a short deadline, yet a must-do. Another phone call informed him that the large order from a single user was going south, and he needed to find out why and resolve it immediately. Obviously the work he had planned to do that morning—a formal report to his immediate boss about the sales progress in his department and the numbers on a specific corporate account, due in his boss's *boss's* office that afternoon—was going to have to wait. Since a prominent feature of Richard's job was the continual reassignment of priorities to the constant stream of demands from clients, coworkers and bosses he received every day, he shifted his morning's priorities with relative ease.

What was not so easy was sitting down to do the actual work on the job that he had deemed most urgent: sketching out his corporate banking client's multitiered project and submitting it to the finance department. It was unreasonable of his client to want a response in such a short time. The finance group was not known for its promptness. Richard tried to concentrate on a request that would convey the urgency he felt, but he couldn't focus his attention completely. He couldn't keep his mind from wandering to other urgent tasks. He even fleetingly imagined the expression on his boss's face when he explained why he had to delay the report. He might even hear a remark about the corporate account information due his boss's own boss.

Since he couldn't fully sink into the massive corporate project with so much on his mind, he called the single-user to find out why they wanted to cancel their order. What that revealed was a hugely complicated situation that had originated in the lower levels of his own company. Plus, the client was angry and Richard had to absorb a great deal of emotional venting over the phone. It took him more than two hours to set it all right. By that time, there were more urgent e-mails and phone calls he hadn't even picked up yet. When he noticed it was lunchtime, the tight muscles in his stomach made it impossible for him to eat. What if he couldn't make this once-prized promotion work out for him?

■ EMMY

Emmy has a regular meditation practice because that's the best way she knows to keep her energy up. And even though she is in her early twenties, Emmy needs lots of energy to fulfill her ambitions. She's in the banking business, and she has every intention of being head of a financial institution someday. Even with the nation's flabby economy, she's right on track. She's an excellent organizer, planner and multitasker. After work she hits the gym to move her body, then has dinner with friends.

She takes several evening classes that reflect her interest in meditation and Buddhist art. On Saturdays she does chores and errands, then treats friends or dates to another of her talents: gourmet cooking. Sundays she's up early, hiking the coastal trails near her home. She loves her life; everything that is important to her is scheduled into it. Except spontaneity. Once she stopped to help an accident victim and it threw off her schedule for days. What's wrong with this picture?

CHAPTER TWO

The Problem of Busyness
Is a Problem of Focus

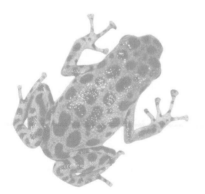

TERMINAL OVERWHELM

Yes, we're all pressured, we're all stressed out! We feel like we might go down any moment, pulled under by the weight of our own tension. The demands of our jobs, the care of our children, our routine chores, our love life (if we're lucky enough to have the time to keep up one—and hopefully with a "low-maintenance" partner), even our exercise, meals, spiritual life and pleasures—the basic sustenance of our beings—combine to give us a feeling of being overwhelmed.

We might not even be able to put aside the unfinished projects at work when we leave for home. A personal assistant made it clear to her boss when she was hired that she couldn't work overtime while her children were still young. But when the chips were down, what did her choice look like in actual experience? She could call a babysitter and then that evening at work—between rushing a proposal from her boss's office to the Xerox department, hunting down the accounts manager in

Atlanta, and booking her boss on an early morning flight—imagine her three-year-old's face falling at the news that Mommy wouldn't be reading him his bedtime story that night. Or alternatively, she could stand firmly by her original contract, call in a temp before going home, and spend the evening with her kids. Between cutting veggies into small pieces and laying out pajamas, reading stories and warming milk, she could worry about whether the temp was good or not and if her job was still secure.

An innovative director of health services at a large hospital had chosen to give his work life the major portion of his energy and creativity—at least until a complementary therapy program he had fostered was stable enough to be run by a new director. He was the one who had the contacts, who could grease the conservative medical wheels enough to make acceptable a hospital-sponsored clinic offering massage, acupuncture and meditation. He promised his wife and two daughters that he would then refocus his attention on his family. His wife, who had a job too, was supportive and proud of her husband's accomplishment. She understood the responsibilities that accompanied a new vision, even though all the logistics of raising a family were left to her: dentist appointments, laundry, school meetings, psychological support and so on. But both spouses believed deeply in service to others. Originally he had asked her for a couple of years. Neither could have pre-dicted how exhausting their lives would become.

They got themselves through this fray day by day, week by week, praying that they had the fortitude to survive until the next weekend, the next vacation, when they could totally crash. They put off the physical maintenance of their bodies and their home, and the psychological maintenance of their friends and extended families, and even each other, until there was a span of time, like a three-day weekend, that felt long enough to think about something else. Then as Sunday midnight approached, signaling a return to work the next day, they flopped down, exhausted, each in his and her own thoughts, just as they had done over the long weekend, each absorbed in his or her own domestic chores, and allowed themselves the satisfaction of the thought that they were caught up at last. Laundry done. Home and children intact.

Then what was that lingering sense of something else that still nagged at her? No, she realized, as the feeling became clearer, it's not something undone. It was the edgy realization that even though everything was done, she still felt uneasy. Because despite all the effort she and her husband had made over the weekend that required all their energy and focus, she, at least, didn't have what she wanted. Even when everything was caught up, contentment still eluded her. Her muscles never completely relaxed; her mind never settled.

It just wasn't fair! After all that effort! She still loved her husband—in theory anyway—but the truth was she couldn't remember what being in love felt like. Now she was only resentful of his putting his clinic ahead of her and the kids. The time to turn his attention back to his family was never quite ripe. The clinic always needed defending, shaping, first aid. She was still doing the lion's share of work at home; he only participated on the occasional three-day weekend. What his wife wanted most now was a few hours of unstructured time in which she might do something besides slump exhausted in front of the TV. She started to fantasize about a South Seas getaway, a meditation retreat in a bucolic setting, or, God love her, even an afternoon having tea and chitchat with old friends. She desperately felt the need to take a break, to get away from her too-busy life in order to refresh herself. She began to include other men in her getaway fantasies and felt guilty about it.

THE PROBLEM IS MANAGING BUSYNESS

Those of us who are self-employed may be the envy of our "wage-slave" friends who tell us we can do anything we want with our time, but the reality of self-employment for many people is the feeling that we can never "clock out" because there's no definite end of work. A friend of mine who has her own small business says, "When you're self-employed, you either have time or money. When you have a lot of work, you're making money but you don't have any time. When you're not working, you have the time for leisurely pursuits, but usually you're too worried about money to enjoy it! It takes a lot of discipline to appreciate what you have now—money or time. The tendency is to worry about what you're missing."

And it isn't that we don't want to be busy. We want to have lives that are interesting and make us feel accomplished and successful. The problem is that we don't know how to *manage* our busyness, to make it function positively as a tune-up to our engines, rather than allowing it to hijack the whole vehicle. In other words, we don't know how to go smoothly from "busy" to "not busy" and back again. We lack the mental flexibility to slip in and out of work mode from moment to moment. The health services director and his wife would have an easier time if they approached some of their routine weekend house chores as opportunities to spend time together: sharing a glass of wine while preparing weekend meals for themselves and their kids; being outside at the same time, in the same physical space at least, while they attend to different house chores. Then, even though they wouldn't be less busy, some of that "busy" time (time still involved in doing chores) could be passed in a "not-busy" way (where there is a lessened sense of the pressure of work to be completed), enjoying each other's good company.

It might be wise to step back for a moment and question the source of our busyness—do we actually have too much to do, or are we just approaching our work too frenetically? Either way, after too long a time of rushed-through chores and hurried kisses good-bye, we find it more and more difficult to give anything our full attention. It's like we've become preoccupied or even shell-shocked in some odd way. Gradually we become aware that we're doing things halfheartedly; we seem incapable of summoning up our concentrated attention without tremendous effort. A real estate agent during the dot-com boom years in San Francisco, when multimillion dollar houses sold as easily as beer at a barbeque, told me he never thought of not working constantly during those years. "Everyone in the business knew it was going to be short-lived, and we had to make hay while the sun shone." After working eighty-hour weeks for more than a year, he was aware that he had become slightly robotic: working hard even though his body was dog-tired; automatically jumping on opportunities that arose without even considering whether their scope merited his effort; eventually not feeling much whether he sold or lost a client. Still he was shocked to notice that his numbness extended to events that he had been looking forward to: his son's recital, a friend's birthday gala, his brother's wedding.

When we become this mechanical and frozen, everything is duller, as if we are closed off by some invisible screen. What we're actually experiencing is an internal neurological mechanism that is shutting us down to protect us from further stimulation. Eventually we might get so numb that we fail to recognize the value inherent in any activity.

It's all the more unsettling when we vaguely suspect that there is actually no real significance to all this busyness—that it is, in fact, pointless, hollow. A software developer, forced during the dot-com boom to drop out of art school to keep up with the demands of his day job, told me, "Sometimes it just seems like a crazy cycle, as if I'm working to afford the labor-saving devices and expensive getaways that enable me to keep working. Sometimes I think that I've allowed myself to get caught up in such a mindless frenzy that I might even be missing the essential point—to be attentive to what I'm actually doing right now." This worker realized how important it is that we do *everything* we do with our whole heart. In this way every activity we perform, special or mundane, becomes inherently nourishing and satisfying for us. And when *we* feel nourished, we want to share our psychological bounty with those around us, to contribute to others' well-being. The inspiring heroes involved in the rescue and comfort of victims of the World Trade Center attack are vivid examples of people contributing to others' well-being and make us less willing to spend our own lives carelessly.

We describe our activity as either "busy" or "not busy," either productively working or taking a blissful break from working. But actually it is possible to experience both "busy" and "not busy" simultaneously, to reach beyond the labels and connect with our work in a way that is deeply satisfying. What this requires is that we develop the breadth of vision and the mental flexibility to be both busy and not busy at the very same time. The Zen teaching we will explore calls this "simultaneous inclusion."

TWO APPROACHES

There are two basic approaches to creating a well-paced and spacious life amidst the pressures and complexities of the working world. The first is to take a break. You can be driven by time and deadlines most of the time and then come up for air by taking a break, like the South American tribe that went on a long walk, day after day, but stopped to rest frequently. They explained that they needed that time of rest so their souls could catch up with them.[2]

The second is by simultaneous inclusion. You can keep your soul with you by doing whatever is in front of you that needs to be done with your whole heart and mind. You can do this most of the time, or at least often enough to make your work and life profoundly gratifying and expressive of your deepest unobstructed nature.

Taking a Break

We all think we know how to do this because this is conceptually very simple. We think of our work life and our leisure life as completely separate. We divide our time into cubicles, with their concomitant psychological attitudes. This activity and mind-set is done here, and that activity and mind-set is done there. For instance, occasionally we stop working. We call this leisure time, a lunch break or vacation time. If we are usually overwhelmed at work, then we think of such breaks as a refuge, as a glimpse of open sky from a crack in an airless cubicle. If we are religious or spiritually inclined, we think of our major weekly break as observing some sort of Sabbath, a regular time set aside for making contact with a different part of our being. We leave workaday thoughts behind and step into the ineffable. The time period involved for a refreshing break or a safe refuge can vary infinitely, all the way from a single breath to an extended sabbatical.

You can allow your soul to catch up with you in the following ways:

- looking up from your desk and gazing out the window
- doing five minutes of movement for every hour on the computer
- taking a day off for unstructured time every week
- attending a five- to thirty-day meditation retreat periodically
- going on a yearly vacation to some relaxing place
- scheduling regular three-day weekend getaways
- taking a long, hot bath
- enjoying a play activity like golf or crossword puzzles
- ringing a mindfulness bell (a bell rung in some monasteries at random intervals that signals a switch of focus from productive activity to just being; at its sound everyone stops whatever they are doing and tunes in to their breath)
- taking a sensory stroll (a walk with no purpose other than receptivity to the senses of sight, smell, hearing and touch)
- doing walking meditation (slow walking in which attention is placed on the muscles and bones of the body parts involved in walking)

- eating a mindfulness meal (a meal in which eating itself—an exclusive awareness of biting, chewing, tasting and swallowing—is the sole focus)

A Break Is a Sabbath

We all think we know how to take a break, but in order to do it successfully—that is, completely shift our full attention from work to something else, and then back to work again later—we have to actually define our "sabbath" space very precisely, as traditional Jews do. The Jewish Sabbath begins at sundown Friday evening and ends at sundown Saturday evening. The times of sundown are set out in the Jewish calendar. It's not a matter of "one more phone call" or "wait till I finish this report." It's a matter of *stopping* whatever we're doing and observing the holy day. If we don't have definite beginning and ending points, we will probably find it very difficult to honor the spirit of this renewal period. The time is meant specifically for stepping out of our usual preoccupation with everyday gaining and losing, striking a different chord in our psyche, one that exposes us to a whole different mode of being. For many of us this will mean going from thinking (linear mode) to simply being (sensing and feeling mode). Changing modes counters our modern tendency to become a one-trick pony—very good at one thing, our job perhaps, but undeveloped in many of the areas that make our lives rich and interesting. Inherently, we're all lovers, poets, artists, caregivers, teachers and free spirits eager for some circumstance that draws an unglimpsed quality out of us. With all these people living inside of us, why should we settle for a monochromatic existence?

In order to build Sabbath-type breaks into one's life and maintain this commitment over the long haul, you have to be very, very convinced of its importance. Old habits are hard to break. It's like starting to exercise regularly. You've got your exercise schedule all set up and you've developed a rhythm that keeps you faithful. Then your in-laws come for a visit. Okay, you'll allow a deviation for the length of that visit; you accept that you have to give over your free time to your relatives while they're here. But a few weeks later, something else comes up, and then something else after that, all of which you feel you have no choice about: a friend's illness, a child's soccer practice, a promotion that will allow you less leisure time but lots more money, and so on.

It may be months before you realize you're way off balance; your whole life now is about meeting obligations. You'd love a long sensory stroll (it used to be built in to your weekly schedule), but there's just no way until the end of next week at least. It's a fact that unless you stay very disciplined and strictly observe your break times—value them as highly as your work times—your tasks will sneak back into dominance of your schedule and overwhelm you as before. Just as a slender pole stuck in the middle of a rushing river will be washed downstream immediately, so will your occasional stabs at creating leisure time for yourself get wiped out by your habit of always putting your work life first. You need to stick that pole in the river over and over again for it to get stout enough to force the current to part around it.

You will be able to master this only by becoming very clear about what you want your life to be and having the discipline to enact it. You'll have to make tough decisions about what you include in your life and what you have to pass on. You'll have to confront your greed, guilt and/or ability to gracefully turn down a request. It may take awhile, perhaps months, to sift through conflicting needs and reaffirm values. You'll have to integrate unexpected events into your life as well. But if you persist, the rewards are great. You'll have the self-knowledge to pursue and enjoy both your work and leisure time with energy and contentment. You'll have a well-balanced life that you sculpted specifically to fit your own needs.

Creating breaks is one way. But there is also another way: simultaneous inclusion.

SIMULTANEOUS INCLUSION

Sometimes just the way we describe our activities is the source of much of our anxiety about how busy we are. For one, we could stop dividing our activity into mental categories that don't serve us, like, for instance, busy/not busy, consequential/trivial. We could stop chopping our time into stress-producing shards of urgent/dispensable, superficial/deep, engrossing/boring. If we knew how to move beyond this judgmental categorization of everything we do, our lives could take on a flowing, nondual quality. From an activity-flow point of view, *every* task we do is inherently valuable, just because it's what we're doing right now. If we're totally intent on what we're doing *right now* and not half here because we're preoccupied with something else, every movement, action and speech is an expression of our full being. We're also not so concerned over whose time we're on—the boss's at work, the kids' at home— resentful that we never seem to have our very own time. We realize that when we stop making these arbitrary divisions in what is actually a seamless expanse of time and movement, it's *all* our own time.

The Zen Approach to Consciousness

The core of the distinction between *taking a break* and *simultaneous inclusion* is contained in the teaching from a venerable Zen *koan*.

Historically, the use of *koans* was one of the distinctive methods employed by various Zen schools. *Koan* literally means "public case" in Japanese. Records of the sayings and doings of earlier Zen masters began to be used as instructional materials and meditation themes. These were not theoretical statements or exercises in intellectual cleverness, as we tend to suppose, but were public cases that people studied as practical tools. *Koans* are not puzzles or riddles. They were designed to confound the habits of intellect, thereby unlocking the user's ability to cross the mental barriers of concept and emerge into direct experience: the perception of the world without our usual conceptual overlay. In our study of learning to focus the attention at will, we will use a traditional Zen *koan* to expedite our passage from focusing sequentially (first on work, then on leisure) to focusing on the flow of activity itself without making distinctions between the kinds of activity we do (simultaneous inclusion).

Traditional *koans* have three parts, each of which is in itself a related teaching: the Introduction, the Case (the main story), and the Commentary added by successive generations of Zen teachers who studied the original teaching and added their own instructions, often in the form of another story or verse.

21st Case, The Book of Serenity
translated by Thomas Cleary

Introduction

Having shed illusion and enlightenment; having cut off holy and ordinary, although there are not so many things, setting up host and guest; and distinguishing noble and mean is a special house. It's not that there is no giving jobs on assessment of ability, but how do you understand siblings with the same breath, adjoining branches?

The Introduction is referring to simultaneous inclusion, or nondual perception, the experience we have when we just do our lives, whatever is under our nose, without considering whether it's timely, boring, pleasant or unpleasant. We just dip our hands into the river of constantly flowing activity and take them out again when it's time to sleep. When we can view our work and leisure—all our activity—this way, we have stopped chopping up our experience into opposing categories. We have shed illusion and enlightenment and cut off holy and ordinary. We've stopped distinguishing noble and mean. "It's not that there is no giving jobs on assessment of ability"—it's not that we can't make any of these distinctions with credibility—but we should remember when we make these distinctions that we are free to *not* make them as well. Feeling oneself free to either distinguish between activities or not distinguish between activities, as the circumstances call for, is "siblings with the same breath, adjoining branches." In other words, it behooves you to be aware that you can experience your activity two ways: you can experience the undifferentiated (nondual or simultaneously included) flow of events on the one hand, and on the other, you can divide activities into categories so that you have the sense of doing one thing after another. Each approach produces a vastly different experience of working, but they have the same source in our minds. We have the choice of how we view the time we spend in activity. We can establish our own reality for ourselves according to which perception, dual or nondual, makes the most sense in any situation.

Case

*As Yunyan was sweeping the ground, Daowu said,
"Too busy."
Yunyan said, "You should know there's one who
isn't busy."
Daowu said, "If so, then there's a second moon."
Yunyan held up the broom and said, "Which
moon is this?"*

In reading traditional Zen teaching stories like this one, you become aware that people who lived in Zen monasteries long ago loved to challenge each other's understanding of the deepest meaning of life. Such activity served as an amusing pastime, a source of satisfying companionship and a means of expanding one's own ability to express the Dharma (a Sanskrit word for the way things work on the most fundamental level; i.e., we can count on the sun rising every morning, the law of gravity, birth, death, Friday afternoon gridlock on the freeway). While Yunyan is doing his sweeping task, Daowu comes up and comments in a critical tone, quite possibly looking for some sport: "You look too busy to be expressing Zen cool to me." Yunyan meets him, pointing out that one can work vigorously without losing one's center: "If you were a mature Zen practitioner, you would realize that appearances are deceiving. Someone can look busy but not have a busy mind." Their swords have been joined. *Touché.*

Daowu continues his provocation: "If so, then there's a second moon." Outrageous. Of course there is no second moon. There's only one moon—one reality. For Zen practitioners, there's no transcendental reality to seek; there is only this, the experience we're having now. (Many religions assume that a more palatable reality exists beyond this one. Zen is radical in that it does not promote or acknowledge any reality other than the one right before us; anything else is merely conceptual and not borne out by our senses.) By referring to a nonexistent "second moon," Daowu is saying, "I'm watching someone who looks busy; are you telling me there's another reality besides the one I see?" Yunyan has fallen into the pit of duality, of assuming a transcendental reality, and so Daowu pounces with his "second moon" wisecrack. Yunyan is indeed down—the referee starts counting: one . . . two . . . three. . . . But don't underestimate Yunyan! He well understands how each of us shapes our own reality according to our point of view. He shakes his broom in Daowu's face and demands, "Which moon is this!" or in other words, "What do you see now, you contemplative idiot? A

broom or a #&!@# idea about moons?" Yunyan thereby dramatically asserted the simultaneity of mundane reality (in
which we distinguish busy from not busy) and nondual reality
(basic awareness in which nothing is differentiated). In the nondual awareness of basic consciousness, our labels are super-
fluous. Zen poets call it "snow in a silver bowl," describing
something where no distinction is possible. In this state of
mind, we aren't conceptualizing about our activity, we are
merely sweeping. Busy and not busy are simultaneously included because we sweep with our full attention. There are no
extraneous thoughts by which to judge our sweeping.

Commentary

. . . 'Without upset there is no solution, without struggle
there is no expression.' Here as Yunyan was sweeping the
ground Daowu casually tested him. Yunyan said, "You
should know there's one who isn't busy." Good people, as
you eat, boil tea, sew and sweep you should recognize the
one who is not busy—then you will realize the union of
mundane reality and enlightened reality; . . . this is called
simultaneous inclusion, naturally not wasting any time.

The phrase "Without upset there is no solution, without struggle there is no expression" asserts the vitality of our lives. Upset and struggle are part of our human lives. When we are beleaguered by demands in the workplace—stressed out from an unbearably high-pressure caseload in a large law firm, going numb in order to keep working through an extended boom time, hysterically revving ourselves up to face a hectic day—we eventually say, "Enough!" and look for a remedy. The Commentary acknowledges that our difficulties often inspire us to exert ourselves to find a better way to do what we have to do, and to have dreams and visions of our relief. Thus we find that right in the middle of our upset, there is our solution, an aspect of the upset itself. Right in the middle of our struggle, we can do no other than express that struggle. However, if we are able to stay alert and attentive during that struggle, solutions will begin to appear. Things are okay; this is the natural process of things.

APPLYING THE TEACHING

So we have the habit of describing our activity as either busy or not busy, either productively working or taking a blissful break from working. On the one hand, we delight in our leisure time as an unstructured idyll of relaxation and ease. In our leisure world we function best by loosening our directed, judgmental mind and switching to a wider, more experiential point of view. Sailing, basking in the sun, reading on the couch or watching a sporting event, we are able to sink more fully into the sensory, feeling realm. The distinctions we make between things and people are not as goal-related as they are at work. On the other hand, in our work and task world, we make an assessment of the worth of objects and activities according to our survival needs. We assign a value to each project and person, and proceed on these judgment calls. In our work world we function by differentiating between activities and people.

Yet it is possible to reach beyond the assigned labels and connect directly with our work in a way that is more deeply satisfying. What this requires is that we develop the breadth of vision and the mental flexibility to "understand siblings with the same breath, adjoining branches." In plain English, both ways of viewing (dual and nondual) have their origin in our minds, and further, they are both ways of viewing the same thing (our activity). So for each of us individually, the practical question becomes, How do we live our lives to simultaneously include the two realms of differentiating and basic nondual awareness in any one activity? When we're new at viewing our activity from the two points of view, we tend to switch back and forth between dual and nondual, trying our skill. This produces a strobe effect: one moment experiencing nondual awareness, the next moment perceiving differences.

In Zen this going back and forth (the strobe effect) between the nondual and the dual realms is often expressed metaphorically with the phrase "when the stone woman gets up to dance." The stone woman represents the nondual realm. She is a solid statue in which nothing moves to differentiate itself. She's all one thing. When she "gets up to dance," the stony monolith breaks up into the many parts we are used to distinguishing. It is much like viewing an oil painting as a canvas . . . and then suddenly perceiving the colors and objects of the oil painting. Then we go back to nondual perception again, perceiving the stone woman as a statue and the painting as a canvas. It is a good attention exercise to go back and forth this way, teaching our brains that our mode of perception can be fluid and adaptable.

The strobe effect may be a stage in training, but simultaneous inclusion—having both points of views simultaneously: dual/nondual, busy/not busy—is what makes our work and life profoundly gratifying and expressive of our most authentic nature. Each realm informs the other. For instance, when we are reclining in a hammock on a summer day, sinking into sensory experience, not labeling or differentiating it, we are basking in the realm of basic awareness. Then when we interrupt the serene surface of the undisturbed pond of our experience to think, "This is a heavenly state of mind," we have switched to the differentiated realm and named and judged our nondual experience. So we come to understand that our perceptions of our states of mind and the things of the world come and go in our experience constantly; we can watch them rise and pass away without undo attachment. At the same time, they are shimmeringly, glisteningly themselves, precious and perfect just as they are.

Each of the two views, both dual and nondual, enhances and informs the other. If we look at our differentiated, relative world from the realm of nondual awareness, each object in the relative world is rendered unique by the possibility of its disappearing into undifferentiated reality. One Zen master said that when he took his teacup down from the shelf, filled it with tea, and drank from it, he very consciously handled it with great reverence and love. In his mind's eye, he could see it broken already, and so it assumed a preciousness and matchlessness that made it unlike any other teacup. This is seeing things as different from one another, while at the same time understanding and accepting that in the realm of direct experience, whatever arises shall eventually pass away.

NECESSARY SKILLS

Everything we do in our professional life can take its rightful place in our daily life if we develop two basic skills that are closely related:

Skill 1: The Ability to Narrow or Widen the Mind's Focus at Will

When we narrow our focus, we give our attention to only one thing, excluding all else that vies for our attention at that time. When we widen our focus, we simultaneously include many things in our attention, aware of the variety of experience rather than the particularity of any one. This enables us to settle our attention deeply and exclusively into any one activity as if it were the *only* activity in the world, then come to the surface where our horizon is broader and place that activity in relation to our general scheme of things. We do this at work when we concentrate on a single aspect of a large project, simultaneously aware of its contribution to the entire program. We do it when we are organizing a complicated project involving charts, phone calls to the sales department for the data, text explanations— which means pulling in a technical writer, scheduling with the Xerox department to have copies made, checking with various assistants to find out where to forward copies and, finally, engaging a typist to write the cover letter. We focus on prepping each task at a time, clarifying it and checking it for errors so carefully that it could easily be the only project, but we also step back and widen our focus to gauge the prep stage of all our individual sections so they will be done at the same time. In another example, we narrow when we listen attentively to our radio in a noisy room, ignoring the other sounds; then with the radio still on, we can also widen our attention to include the other sounds in the room.

Skill 2: The Mental Flexibility to Shift the Mind's Focus at Will from One Thing to Another

This means, in other words, to go from "narrow" to "narrow" to "narrow" quickly; to completely let go of one object of focus and completely take up another. Some objects of attention are very compelling, like an annoying noise or a stabbing pain in your body. We are especially likely to get stuck in compulsive and repetitive thinking when we are anxious about something and we become unable to shift the focus of our attention from fear to some other more helpful aspect of the situation. But if we learn the skill to shift our attention at will, we increase our options in difficult situations exponentially. We are no longer at the mercy of a single point of view. Standing frantically by the copy machine while focused on the progress of a report toward its deadline fosters a very different quality of attention than does observing the intricacies of the office flower arrangement on a nearby desk as the copy machine churns out the work.

Having the mental flexibility to shift the mind's focus means that when it seems as if there's way too much to do, we simply do our work—mindfully absorbed in our actions and thoughts. When it's lunchtime, we eat lunch with the same kind of absorption and devotion we gave our demanding work. When the workday is over, we go home and give our children, our spouse and our leisure the same kind of attention: an attitude that what is before us is the whole world. When we sink deeply into our activity, whatever that activity is, everything is simultaneously included at the same time. The grief we once felt over a life incompletely lived, squandered on the demands of others and trivial chores, is transformed into a deep feeling of fulfillment and a flexibility up to meeting any stimulus.

HOW MULTITASKING REALLY WORKS

Many people report the frustration of multitasking; that is, doing several separate activities at once: eating, working on the computer, talking to a coworker on the phone. It's annoying because we're quite aware that nothing is getting done well, and the overriding experience of doing everything at once gives us a frantic, helpless feeling. We know we shouldn't multitask at all, but we feel that if we didn't do a couple of needling things at once, we'd never get them done at all!

Again, the problem is one of focus, not activity level. Usually when we multitask, we're focused on what we're *not* doing, not what our hands are actually doing that moment. We stay in perception of the whole and don't settle into any one activity because we're shifting so frequently. Whenever we experience this kind of frustration and anxiety, we might find relief by matching our focused awareness with the motions that our hands or our bodies are actually doing at that moment. This way we feel the alignment between our attention and motions, which is a much more satisfying feeling (it "just feels right") than when we are paying attention to something our hands aren't doing. After a few seconds of "narrow" concentration, using the skill of widening the mind's focus at will, we rise above the fray, instantaneously assess each task's progress, then settle our attention again onto what we're actually doing with our hands.

So why don't we just do this automatically, simultaneously including the realms of differentiation and nondual awareness in whatever we're doing? Aren't these states of mind our birthright? They are indeed our birthright—they come with the human brain—but our brains are infinitely malleable, and as such they are very vulnerable to education and cultural conditioning. Our culture puts a great deal of emphasis on the end result of activity and motion; we don't educate ourselves to notice the way we get there. Work that produces goods and services and leads to the consumption of them is the most important thing. Being goal-oriented most of the time requires that we lead our life from our "head." Our ideas, our plans and our expectations are what we pay most attention to, rather than our feelings or the sensations of our body. Our body basically becomes the mobile equipment that gets us across the street and to our appointments. Our ideas about our abilities and what we ought to accomplish are what we focus on in our daily life. Given this disproportionate emphasis on tangibles, we have gradually allowed our primal connections to other things, like our bodies and our subtle feelings, to be discounted and mechanized. We don't "waste time" sitting in the sun unless we're already "useless" in some way. Interpersonal relationships have been compromised by the cultural need to achieve and compete. Spiritual ties, which I define as a belief in some reality beyond the material world, have for many people been severed altogether.[3]

So this is not the best environment in which to rely on our

innately human abilities to sense and feel the world around us without categorizing its parts into separate concepts. Try looking at a city block as if it were a still life, a whole portrait. Resist the conditioning that has taught you to see separate things: houses, cars, streets and sidewalks. This is very difficult to do, to see things without our preconceived notions of what they are and what they are for. We need special training to be able to fade in and out of nondual awareness at will and to include it as part of our daily experience.

CHAPTER THREE

Exercises That Cultivate
the Skill of Simultaneous Inclusion

In order to develop the ability to perceive the simultaneous inclusion that this Zen *koan* teaches, we must provide opportunities for both our discriminating mind and our unbounded nondual awareness (our "sensory mind") to arise together so that we can be informed by both. As we get better at focusing our thoughts on what we wish to focus on, we will experience our work activities and the demands of our livelihood in a much more spacious way.

The first thing we need to do before we do any special training is to get an accurate idea of how our own basic consciousness behaves when left to its own devices. The following exercise will give us a clear picture of our mind's strong tendency to return again and again to its long-standing habits—compulsive list-making; restlessness, anxious thoughts; critical judgment; whatever that is for you personally—unless we teach it to widen or narrow the focus it already has in order to take in many aspects of a situation.

■ PRACTICE 1:

WANDERING MIND MEDITATION: SITTING STILL AND COUNTING THE BREATH FROM 1–10

Object of Focus: the various excursions our mind takes away from counting the breaths.

1. Arrange yourself in a position that is both stable and comfortable.

2. Settle yourself and begin to notice your breath, specifically the inhalations and exhalations.

3. Without changing the natural rhythm of your breath, begin to count the inhalations and exhalations from one to ten. An inhalation and an exhalation count as one breath; that is, the first time you breathe in, you say "one" in your mind; when you breathe out, you say "one" again. The next inhalation is "two;" the next exhalation is "two."

4. When you get to "ten," start over again so that you are counting a continuous series of one to ten. Continue this throughout your period of meditation—say, for fifteen, twenty, or thirty minutes.

Whenever your attention leaves your counting, note specifically where it goes—to what you have to do after this period of meditation, to a fantasy of what you'd rather be doing, to thoughts of irritation or agitation or sleepiness, to a work project, whatever. It doesn't matter where it goes. What's important is that you gently return it to your breath and your counting. The counting is to help you notice that your attention has strayed. What may be especially interesting to you is where it goes. You may notice obsessive patterns and habits of mind you weren't aware of before starting this practice. No matter how many times you lose track of your counting, note where your attention goes, over and over again, and then gently bring it back to your counting. The *Wandering Mind Meditation* both develops your ability to focus your mind at will and reveals your own particular habits of mind, the favorite places you revisit again and again, the places you'd rather be than where you actually are.

To continue our training, we must take the kind of skill we began to cultivate in the *Wandering Mind Meditation*—the ability to focus our minds on a particular object (in this case our breathing)—and apply it to a more fluid situation, where there is dynamic stimulation, namely, when we are moving. We are usually moving in our work and task life whether we are using our body to do a chore or sitting at a desk using our hands and eyes. Most of the time we ignore the sensations in our body caused by our movements because they seem irrelevant to finishing our task. But in doing so, we overlook an enormous resource for the perception of refuge and spaciousness in our daily lives.

Our rational, thinking minds are brilliant, amusing and incredibly useful. No wonder we spend so much time in our thoughts, as we saw in the *Wandering Mind Meditation!* But our rational mind is like the self-absorbed potentate of a tiny kingdom. The true wisdom and virtually limitless breadth of vision available to us as human beings lies in the integration of our body/minds, in allowing the world of feelings and sensory awareness to penetrate our thoughts and ideas. Our senses don't care about our mortgage or our neighbor's new car. They are indifferent to deadlines and the quarterly report. Body sensations don't care about "busy." They only perceive what's here; they don't worry about what's not. And because our feelings and bodily awareness tend to arise from deeper needs than our ego's dictates, they make excellent consultants, sanctuaries and priority setters. So if we develop the mental flexibility to drop into this ocean of peace and value at will, to integrate the information it provides into the flow of our conceptual thoughts, we will effectively enrich our workday world. Awareness of feelings and sensations arising from the body represents the nondual awareness that we wish to integrate into our dualistic, or differentiating, thinking minds. The following exercises introduce body awareness into everyday consciousness. When we speak of simultaneous inclusion—of integrating nondual awareness and the differentiating mind—we are speaking of developing the ability to perceive body consciousness and conceptual mind simultaneously. First we must be able to summon awareness of the body with reliable ease.

FOCUS ON YOUR ACTIVITY

It is very important when undergoing the training set forth in this book that we be patient with ourselves. We are dealing with habits that are not only nearly as old as we are, but also strongly reinforced by our culture. An economy based on consumerism has a huge stake in distracting us from our worries by promoting short-term delight in a new possession. To maximize our consumer spending, desirable products must replace each other, one after another, as quickly as possible. Thus, we are encouraged to attend to our surroundings very briefly and superficially, but the training to comprehend simultaneous inclusion takes us in the opposite direction. We are training our minds to focus on something long enough to begin to be able to bring other aspects into that focus as well, to apprehend different facets of reality at exactly the same time. You won't learn this watching MTV. You will learn something about absorbing retinal images quickly by watching MTV, which has its own value, but you will not learn to add layers of dimension to your daily perception there.

So please be patient with yourself. Don't be in a hurry. Just do the exercises for their own sake if you find them pleasant, and let the process take its own time. It helps if you can resist being goal-oriented, if you can just relax and enjoy the training itself with its little epiphanies. It will begin immediately to enrich your understanding of reality because the training literally expands your consciousness. Your primary mental hangout may be in your ideas, your plans or your thoughts, and you may experience feelings of fear, pain or pleasure in your body only occasionally. In your case, the training will bring sensory awareness and different levels of conceptualization to your experience. If you find the chores in your life flat and tiresome, you will be delighted to discover the layers of consciousness that await you in even the most repetitious activities.

■ PRACTICE 2:

MEDITATION ON MOVEMENT

Exercises 1–6: Body Awareness

Object of Focus: sensations of the body as a reliable refuge from the perception of busyness.

Even though you have a big deadline and a mortgage to pay, your body doesn't really care. Your body, on the contrary, actually gets restless and irritated by your anxieties and concerns. It responds by tensing and contracting when it would rather be pumping blood and stretching its muscles. Because your body has no interest in your coworker's snit or your upcoming promotion, it is an extremely reliable place to go for solace and peace. When you start getting wound up and anxious, you can include your body's equanimity in your emotional viewpoint. And once you've learned how, you can drop into its sensations in a heartbeat, then return to your thinking mind in another heartbeat, refreshed. If you can get in touch with the sensations of your body, sitting still or moving, you may suddenly feel all the profoundly nourishing connections that your ordinary life does not include, like the fact that you sit on this planet earth, that your breath goes in and out continuously, that your bones shift when you change your posture and so on.

If you are new to the skill of feeling the sensations of your body as it moves, you will benefit from doing specific movements that increase your ability to feel the motion of your body in your everyday activities. The best kind of awareness exercises are those that involve gentle movements, slowly done, so that the brain can easily track the movement you do, and you can therefore feel the sensations that arise in your muscles and joints. While you are attending to your precise bodily sensations, which are the focus of these movements, you begin to experience the tension between thought and sensation. In order to feel the intricacies of your movement, you must stop thinking long enough to feel sensation. When you follow a train of thought, you have to ignore your sensations and put your body on automatic pilot. You must do one or the other. This is how movement can soothe muscles contracted with tension and calm a mind frantic with stress. You drop past the tension and stress into the sensation of movement.

These exercises will train your consciousness to include sensory information. They are done slowly and precisely enough that your attention can stay on your sensations and your feelings as they are evoked by the small movements that you do. The sequence of movements helps you notice very small differences in the feelings of adjacent muscle groups. Doing these movements, you are thoroughly engaged with bodily sensation, which is a strong antidote to discursive thought.

■ EXERCISE 1: BIG TOE TURN

1. Sit on a chair low enough so that your feet easily reach the floor. Stretch your legs out straight in front of you with only your heels on the floor.

2. Wiggle your toes and become aware of your feet. Place your feet at least a foot apart from each other.

3. Turn your big toes toward each other, being careful to turn only your feet. Don't use your leg, thigh or hip muscles to turn. Feel only your big toes turn toward each other, pulling the rest of the foot along.

4. Release your feet and let them fall away from each other.

5. Repeat again and then again. As you move your big toes toward each other and then release your feet so that they fall away, notice the movement and therefore the sensation this causes in your hips. Your hips are passively moved because your feet cause them to turn in the joint. This exercise teaches your brain the difference between effort (when you turn your toes toward each other) and release (when you allow your toes to fall away from each other).

■ EXERCISE 2: MOVE HEAD FROM SIDE TO SIDE

1. Sit in a comfortable chair with feet on the floor (or rungs of chair) and back supported against the back of the chair. Rest your hands on your knees.

2. Breathe deeply a few times. Then begin to move your head from side to side very slowly and in a way that does not demand anything from the neck muscles. Feel as if someone else had your chin in their hand and is moving your chin from side to side. Stay well within your full range of movement; allow your head to feel very loose. In other words, stay within the range of movement that allows you to perceive the looseness of your neck rather than its limitations.

3. Continue to move your head from side to side until you can differentiate the weight of your head at different loci in the arc of your movement. Follow the sensation of the movement as far as it goes into your neck and shoulders.

■ EXERCISE 3: LOWER ARMS AROUND ELBOW

1. Sit comfortably on a chair, resting your elbows on the arms of the chair. If your chair has no arms, then just rest your elbows loosely against the sides of your body with your arms hanging comfortably from your shoulders. Breathe in and out a few

times, feeling your abdomen expand and contract with the air.

2. Begin to rotate your hands and forearms around your elbows, both arms at the same time. Your fingertips should lead the motion of your forearms around your elbow; allow your wrists to be loose. Your fingers are active and moving. Feel their effort as you move. Feel the tips of your fingers contact the cool air. Feel the bottom of your fingers where they join your palm. Continue to breathe and feel the sensations produced by your rotation in your fingers, hands, arms and anywhere else the movement reaches. Notice any sensations this rotation produces in your upper torso or any changes it effects in your breathing pattern after awhile.

■ EXERCISE 4: STRETCH ARM ACROSS TABLE

1. Sit on a chair so that your feet rest securely on the floor and face your desk or a table.

2. Stretch your straight arms out from your shoulders across the desk, allowing your head and upper body to rest on the desk as well.

3. Continue to stretch your arms out across the desk as far as you are able, feeling the sensation spread out across your upper back and shoulders as you stretch.

■ Exercise 5: Rock Pelvis in Chair

1. Sit in a chair with your feet on the ground. It is not necessary to sit away from the back of the chair. You can rest your spine on the back of the chair.

2. Put the back of your hand on the last (lower-most) three vertebrae in your lower back. These are the vertebrae you want to move.

3. Now relax those vertebrae completely (slump in the chair without trying to hold yourself up).

4. Now contract the muscles around those vertebrae so that your whole upper body is straightened and lifted by the action of these muscles. Don't use any other muscles of your upper body. Allow the lower vertebrae of your back to do all the work.

5. Continue to alternately relax and contract these three lumbar vertebrae so that you have a fluid, rocking motion in your lower back, which lifts and releases your upper body.

■ Exercise 6: Raise and Lower Bent Legs

1. Sit on the edge of a chair so that your feet are securely on the ground, your knees comfortably apart.

2. Lift your right leg (knee bent) off the ground, continuing

as high as your leg will comfortably go, then let your leg sink back down gently to the ground. Think of your foot as leading your leg through its various positions up and down.

3. Repeat with your left leg.

4. Continue to alternate your left and right legs, raising and lowering them and feeling the multitude of sensations produced in your hips, lower back, knees, legs and feet.

Exercises 7–10: Mental Flexibility
(the ability to integrate ever more
complicated events into the attention)

Object of Focus: A single focal point into which movements in different parts of the body are integrated at once.

You begin by doing a movement in a particular part of the body, and then add another movement in another part of the body, and so on until you are doing four or five movements at one time. Each additional movement requires a further shift toward integration of body and brain because neither can handle the coordination of movement without the other. This provides a direct experience of the mental flexibility required to join body and mind in everyday activity, a physical "taste" of simultaneous inclusion.

■ EXERCISE 7: LEG ROTATIONS

1. Sit back in your chair so as to allow some distance between your feet and the floor. If this is difficult because you have long legs, add a pillow or phone book to your chair so that your feet clear the floor.

2. Rotate your lower legs around your knees so that your legs are moving together in the same direction, both of them making a circle to the right.

3. Change direction and rotate both legs to the left.

4. Separate your knees a little more and begin to rotate your lower legs in opposite directions so that each leg moves away from each other as it rotates.

5. Again rotate your legs in the same direction, first to the right and then to the left. Again rotate each of them in the opposite direction from the other.

6. For a final challenge, rotate your ankles at the same time that you rotate your lower legs in same and different directions.

■ EXERCISE 8: ARMS AND BELLY COORDINATION

1. Sit on the edge of a chair so that your feet are solidly on the floor and your back is straight.

2. Take a deep breath; on the out-breath, lift your right arm forward and up alongside your right ear, keeping your arm straight. Try to lead this motion with your fingers and hand so that you can feel your shoulder and neck area relax.

3. Inhale while your straight arm is up alongside your ear.

4. When you next breathe out, put your right arm back down at the same time you lift your left arm forward and up alongside your left ear.

5. Inhale while your straight left arm is up alongside your ear.

6. When you next breathe out, put your left arm back down at the same time that you lift your right arm forward and up alongside your right ear. Continue to alternate your arms whenever you breathe out.

7. After your arm alternation is well established, begin to suck your belly in and then push it out as you raise and lower your arms. Let your breath continue normally; don't change it to accommodate your abdominal movement. Alternately contract and extend your abdominal muscles so that your belly goes in and out while you are moving your arms. Feel the independence of your belly and your arms while you do these two movements. See if you can notice how it is you are able to do two movements independently at once. Is your brain responsible? Is your body doing it automatically? See if you can trace this ability to its source.

■ EXERCISE 9: SEPARATION OF ARMS AND LEGS

1. Sit on the edge of a chair so that your feet are solidly on the floor and your back is straight.

2. Take a deep breath; on the out-breath, lift your right arm up alongside your right ear, keeping your arm straight. Try to lead this motion with your fingers and hand, so that you can feel your shoulder and neck area relax.

3. Inhale while your straight arm is up alongside your ear.

4. When you next breathe out, put your right arm back down at the same time you lift your left arm forward and up alongside your left ear.

5. Inhale while your straight left arm is up alongside your ear.

6. When you next breathe out, put your left arm back down at the same time you lift your right arm forward and up alongside your left ear. Continue to alternate your arms whenever you breathe out.

7. When your arm movement is well established, begin to rotate your lower legs around your knees at the same time that you move your arms. Continue to breathe normally. Sometimes rotate your lower legs around your knees in the same direction, sometimes in the opposite direction from each other. Do the motions so that you feel the independence of your arms and legs; they feel very separated from each other in their movement.

8. When your arm and leg motions are well established, try to add rotating your feet around your ankles at the same time that you rotate your lower legs. As in the previous exercise, try to find the locus of your ability to coordinate these movements. Do you find it in mind or body? Or are they indistinguishable now? Is breath involved?

■ Exercise 10: Whole Body Coordination

1. Sit on the edge of a chair so that your feet are securely on the ground, your knees comfortably apart.

2. Breathe in and out a few times, feeling your abdomen expand and contract with the air. Bend your elbows and rest them loosely against the sides of your body with your arms hanging comfortably from your shoulders.

3. Rotate your lower arms around your elbows very slowly so that you can feel the change in your wrists and lower arm muscles as you do this. Let your fingers lead the motion of your arms around your elbows, which also increases the feeling in the wrists and hands. Continue this rotation for several minutes.

4. When the rotation of your elbows is well established, begin to slowly move your head from side to side. Allow your neck to relax completely. Move slowly and gently enough that

62

THE ONE WHO IS NOT BUSY

you don't feel tension in your neck. Breathe deeply to encourage the separation between the movements of your head and your lower arms.

5. When the movements of your upper body (your head and elbow rotation) are well established, lift your right leg (knee bent) off the ground, continuing as high as your leg will comfortably go, then let your leg sink back down gently to the ground. Think of your foot as leading your leg through its various positions up and down.

6. Repeat with your left leg. Alternate lifting and lowering your bent legs at the same time that you rotate your lower arms around your elbows and turn your head from side to side.

7. Now you are doing five movements at once: Rotating both arms, turning your head, alternating your leg movement and breathing! See if you can add one more: opening and closing your mouth. Open and close your mouth in the same slow, steady rhythm that you move your head.

Expanding Our Mental Landscape at Work

In doing these coordination exercises, we begin to understand how we could focus on our work and the sensations of our body simultaneously, thereby expanding our mental landscape beyond our usual narrow preoccupation with getting things done. These exercises are challenging; they require the kind of mental flexibility that continually absorbs and digests new information on various levels of our being, very similar to the constant challenge of absorbing new tasks, information and personalities in a stimulating workplace. It doesn't serve us to block out new facts, new people, and innovative approaches because we are overwhelmed by all the constant change. We adapt better and feel much more stimulated and gratified in a creative environment if we have trained ourselves to be flexible in our focus. It's like MTV with dimension!

The more we are able to consciously direct the focus of our thoughts, the more options we have for how we experience our work activities. We can choose to focus first on, say, the planning of our morning's tasks; then as we do our tasks, we can simultaneously include the body's point of view. There are a multitude of potential objects of focus in any given situation. The better we get at noticing them and discerning the most helpful, the more sources of information we have available for decision-making (widening our focus) and the greater array from which to choose an object of focus that may influence our state of mind (narrowing our focus).

■ PRACTICE 3:

WALKING MEDITATION
WITH DIFFERENT OBJECTS OF FOCUS

This exercise develops the two capacities that are crucial to experiencing simultaneous inclusion: the ability to narrow or widen the focus of the mind at will and the mental flexibility to shift the mind's focus from one thing to another.

Choose an area in which you can walk clockwise in a large circle. A garden is, of course, perfect, but a medium-sized cubicle will do if that's what you have to work with. Walk more slowly than you usually do when you're trying to get somewhere, more like a saunter. Arrange your arms in a particular way, perhaps down at your side or with fingers interlaced in front of you. It helps to focus if you feel quietly contained in this practice rather than "any ol' way." Rest your gaze on the ground about three to six feet ahead of your body. As you walk, you will feel pleasantly enclosed within this practice.

The focus of your attention will also reflect this containment. As you walk, you will be able to practice focusing your mind exclusively on a single instruction that will change every four minutes. To avoid constantly looking at a clock, set a timer for four minutes every time you change the object of focus. The objects of focus are as follows:

1. Number of Steps Per Breath

As you breathe in and out normally, count the number of steps you take as you do so. With your gaze still on the ground in front of you, count the number of steps you take during an entire inhale and exhale. Start your counting at "one" every time you inhale. Every time another kind of thought begins to intrude, gently bring your attention back to counting the number of steps you are taking as you inhale and exhale.

2. Muscle and Bone

With your gaze still on the ground in front of you, focus your attention exclusively on the muscles and bones of your lower body as you shift your weight from one foot to the other, one side of your lower body to the other. You will feel the sensations of your muscles as you use them to support your bones at all points of your walking. Notice these sensations. Every time another kind of thought begins to intrude, gently bring your attention back to your muscles and your bones.

3. Sense of Touch

This time you are paying attention only to what you feel against your skin. This will be the touch of your clothes, your shoes, the ground against your feet, the air, the breeze, your hair, jewelry—whatever comes into contact with your skin.

Keep your gaze on the ground in front of you. Every time another kind of thought begins to intrude, gently bring your attention back to your skin.

4. Sounds

With your gaze still on the ground in front of you, give your complete attention to hearing the sounds inside and outside of your body, inside and outside of your room, every sound you can hear. Resist labeling these sounds; don't give them a name. Just hear them without knowing what they are. Hear them begin and end separately and overlap each other without thinking about where they come from. Every time another kind of thought begins to intrude, gently bring your attention back to what you hear.

5. Perception of Color and Form

Raise your gaze from the ground and look all around you. Try seeing what's around you in terms of color and form, not in terms of what the objects are used for or what we normally call them. In other words, see "red" and a particular shape, not "house," "chair," "wall," "person," "lamp." This will be especially interesting if you are able to walk outside. This practice is not easy, by the way, so be especially patient with yourself on this one. We have been trained from childhood to label things. The trouble with doing this all the time, though, is that we learn to label them and then we dismiss them. We don't really experience them as if for the first time. They're safely in their categories. We no longer see their individuality or their uniqueness. They're just another lamp, another chair. Every time a distracting thought or a category of things begins to intrude, gently bring your attention back to what you're actually seeing with your bare eyes. What this practice will do for you is wake up your senses. You will learn to actually *look* at something, not just perceive it. Colors take on a new vibrancy; objects take on some vital quality we haven't noticed since childhood. But these are just the side effects of this particular practice. You will be learning, over time, to switch your object of focus whenever you wish and sink deeply into whatever it is. You are learning the skill of concentrating briefly but intensely, a skill as useful to life in our contemporary world as any computer skill you have. Practice this color-and-form exercise as often as you can, when you're walking to work or walking for pleasure. It's a difficult skill to attain but useful and fun to attempt.

6. *Notice What You Don't Like to Look At*

Raise your gaze from the ground and look all around you, as you did in the last practice. Notice what you don't like and would change if you could. Perhaps there's some garbage on the street, a crack in the plaster in your room or a pile you haven't straightened out. Every time a distracting thought begins to intrude, gently bring your attention back to your judgments of what is not pleasing in your environment.

7. Notice What You Do Find Aesthetically Pleasing

Raise your gaze from the ground and look all around you, as you did in the last practice. Notice what pleases you, what is beautiful or symmetrical. It might be a plant, a picture, a color or an arrangement. Every time another kind of thought begins to intrude, gently bring your attention back to your judgments of what is pleasing in your environment.

Practicing these exercises, we learn to focus our attention on our body, breath and sense impressions. By focusing on the bare data that our eyes see, we subvert the usual ways we organize our seen world, and through picking out what we like or dislike in an arbitrary way, we become aware of our habitual critical judgments, negative or positive. Acquiring the ability to focus sequentially at will and to narrow or widen the focus as demanded by the object of concentration dramatically increases our sense of richness and, at the same time, gives us some useful perspective on our habits of mind. Finally, we learn to test and refine our ability to integrate our body awareness with our thinking, judging brain.

■ PRACTICE 4:

TALKING MEDITATION

Object of Focus: Breathing and communicating simultaneously.

In any conversation, short or long, tune in to your own breath at least three times while (1) listening to another person speak, and (2) while you yourself are talking. This is another practice that is directly contrary to how we have been taught to have a conversation, so it is difficult to learn but very rewarding. The key is absolute patience with yourself. Don't rate yourself, judge yourself or create any expectations of your performance. Just notice that you are breathing while giving attention to what another person is saying. When you are practicing the second part of the exercise, notice that you are breathing while you are organizing the thoughts that enable you to speak coherently. If it's a long enough conversation, do it three separate times— three times while they're talking and three times while you're talking. Try it while talking on the phone.

This is true simultaneous inclusion. You are thinking and feeling your breath at the same time. Some people have been concerned that tuning into the breath takes you out of the conversation for a few seconds and shortchanges the other person, but it's not so. Your breath gives you the distance you need from the conversation in order to participate in it from real interest rather than from habitual conditioning. If your friend is telling you something emotionally demanding, awareness of your breath will help you bring your feelings forward. It may even enable you to be a fully attentive witness to your friend's suffering rather than a knee-jerk giver of advice. Most people are not telling you their troubles in order to hear your advice. Giving advice is usually a strategy to keep a friend's pain at bay.

■ PRACTICE 5:

EATING MEDITATION

Object of Focus: Tasting, chewing and swallowing.

While eating a meal, once a day or every meal, choose one portion or dish that you will eat mindfully. Eating mindfully means that you eat with full attention to the tastes and sensations of eating. Tastes are registered at different areas of the mouth. You may become aware of these. Every food has numerous textures, which contributes to our pleasure and food preferences. Notice whether you chew more on one side of your mouth than the other. Follow the sensations of the food being swallowed until you lose track of it down your throat. Become aware of when you perceive the feeling of fullness and don't need to eat any more food.

This kind of practice brings the pleasure inherent in many of our everyday activities to our attention. We only need to be fully present as we do them to reap the bounty they contain. Many people hate to do laundry, wash the dishes, vacuum. They consider such routine chores an imposition on their already busy lives. But they overlook the potential refuge of such simple tasks from the harried state of mind that accompanies many more complex activities. If we become aware of our senses and body sensations while we fold laundry—the smell of clean linens, the stretch of our arm muscles to fold sheets, the intrinsic satisfaction of creating several neat piles—we can escape from the anxiety of complexity and into the sensuous pleasure of simple tasks. We can find peace in the warm water running over our hands in the sink as we wash dishes or the revelation of a china pattern as the debris floats clear. Such tiny delights. It takes a refined consciousness to revel in them, to discover there a safe haven from the demands of the day. Eating and laundry meditations cultivate that kind of consciousness.

CHAPTER FOUR

Training the Busy Ones

■ NANCY

Nancy was extremely discouraged to realize that quitting the large law firm and doing freelance brief writing at home still had not given her a feeling of control over her time. When her husband got home that evening, she sat him down, poured them each a glass of wine, and told him she knew she was not only driving herself crazy but putting their marriage in jeopardy as well. The need to produce "perfect" work overrode her wish to take romantic trips with her husband and cultivate deeper relationships with relatives and friends. Although she valued these latter pursuits highly, she could not seem to break her lifetime habit of perfection. They discussed it through the evening, and her husband, while affirming support for Nancy's career, expressed his own wish to have a wife and companion with whom he could share his leisure time. Though she was extremely attached to her job, Nancy began to think she would have to stop working in order to save her marriage.

As it turned out, she didn't have to give up her work. The solution she came to was internal. After taking a class in simultaneous inclusion, she decided it was unwise to spend time trying to get rid of her compulsive self—it was so powerful—but thought she might be able to integrate other aspects of herself into it. She needed to cultivate *Skill 1: The ability to narrow or widen the mind's focus at will.* This would help her cultivate the ability not only to settle her attention deeply and exclusively into her casework as if it were the only activity in the world, but also to come to a wider perspective when she wanted to and place her casework where she really valued it in relation to her marriage and personal life. She began doing several of the exercises related to *Practice 2: Meditation on Movement (Object of Focus: sensations of the body as a reliable refuge from the perception of busyness).* What she learned about focusing on her body from the body awareness exercises, she applied to the movements of her daily life. Whenever she needed to get a cup of tea, sharpen a pencil or retrieve a file, she shifted the focus of her attention from the purpose of her errand to her body parts as they moved to carry her around the room.

A walk on the beach was already part of her daily schedule, but too often she had been unable to get her mind off her work during the walk. She began using her beach walk to practice a particular portion of *Practice 3: Walking Meditation with Different Objects of Focus,* which proved useful to someone as conceptually oriented as she was, namely, the practice of resisting the habit of organizing her sight perceptions into familiar objects as she walked, but instead noticing color and form only. So instead of seeing houses and dogs and ocean and sky, she saw different-colored rectangles and scampering brown bundles of energy and a huge expanse of gray-blue towering over another huge expanse of gray-green movement.

■ LUANN

LuAnn couldn't continue viewing everything in her life—being with her kids, planning meals, even making love to her husband—as a chore. That way lay bitterness and despair. So she had to consider her choices. In her determination to resume her professional standing, was she shortchanging her family and herself? Should she stop working until her children were older? After taking a class in simultaneous inclusion as part of the Stress Reduction Program that I taught at her local hospital, LuAnn decided to try to keep working *and* mothering, just as she was, but change her self-defeating attitude. Instead of focusing on work and trying to slip in housework around the edges, she thought she could stop making such sharp distinctions between work and home. That way, her days—every moment of them filled with unceasing activity—could take on a more flowing quality.

She began doing *Practice 1: Wandering Mind Meditation: Sitting Still and Counting the Breath from 1–10 (Object of Focus: the various excursions our mind takes away from counting the breaths)* and *Practice 2: Meditation on Movement (Object of Focus: sensations of the body as a reliable refuge from the perception of busyness).* Like Nancy did, she began to generalize the movement training to the moving part of her daily chores, both at work and at home. She spent some time at her desk between projects twisting her big toes toward each other *(Body Awareness Exercise 1)* and rocking her pelvis in her chair *(Body Awareness Exercise 5).* The exercises seemed to center her deeply and clear her mind for the next project.

■ KEN

The pressure on Ken to come up with a steady stream of original ideas all day and then face his energetic girlfriend at night was starting to affect his health. He needed to make decisions about what was most important to spend his energy on. He had plenty of it but tended to work until he was exhausted, then go home too tired for any other pursuits. This was putting his relationship with his girlfriend in jeopardy. Plus, he seemed to be oblivious to the amount of stress his body absorbed day after day. It was breaking down, expressing the vulnerability he did not register consciously. He was referred to my Stress Reduction class by his osteopath. When I suggested that he start practicing at home the meditation we did in the group—*Practice 1: Wandering Mind Meditation: Sitting Still and Counting Your Breath from 1–10 (Object of Focus: the various excursions our mind takes away from counting the breaths)* in order to become more familiar with the way his mind worked, he protested that he didn't have time to do what he already *had* to do, let alone some senseless exercise! I asked him, then, to pay particular attention to that exercise while he was in class. It didn't surprise me when he volunteered two weeks later to do *Practice 1* at home as I had originally suggested. He was a very bright, curious man, and I knew he would find his own mind fascinating. He not only enjoyed observing his own random thoughts and feelings during meditation, but he soon began to be captivated by the possibilities inherent in the apparently inexhaustible malleability of the human mind.

Since his doctor suspected the genesis of his back problems to be emotional stress, I asked Ken to widen his focus during his workday to include the various emotions he had—the feelings of exaltation, frustration, fear and disappointment that accompanied his progress from original idea, to working with others in their development, and finally to the project's evaluation by his superiors. Ken began doing *Practice 4: Talking Meditation (Object of Focus: breathing and communicating simultaneously)*, tuning in to his feelings during his product evaluation discussions with his bosses after he had presented his most recent creations. It was very hard for him to widen his focus this way, but he was persistent. At first his shifts were cumbersome and distracting from the business of the evaluation; he missed some of the conversation by abruptly focusing on his feeling. But as he practiced, he became more deft, and finally his shifts were not distracting at all.

■ MICHAEL

Michael finally pinned the blame for his lack of work satisfaction on his revving habit itself. Yet when he tried hard to extend his morning meditation feeling into the workplace, he was impressed with how persistent his habit of urgent overkill was, even when he wanted to break it. He apparently believed that without that kind of urgency, no work would ever get done. He needed to learn *Skill 2: The Mental Flexibility to Shift the Mind's Focus At Will from One Thing to Another* to completely let go of one object of focus and completely take up another, rather than continue his habit of seeing everything all at once and getting frantic about taking care of it all instantaneously. He needed to go sequentially from activity to activity all day long, steadily applying himself to each one. To this end, he began to train himself with three of the simultaneous inclusion practices: *Practice 3: Walking Meditation with Different Objects of Focus,* which would require him to focus totally on one aspect of his environment, and then to shift his focus to another one in a short amount of time; *Practice 4: Talking Meditation (Object of Focus: breathing and communicating simultaneously),* integrating two foci at the same time; and *Practice 5: Eating Meditation (Object of Focus: tasting, chewing and swallowing),* training him to concentrate deeply on the single activity of eating.

After a few weeks of practicing these skills and noticing his effort in numerous work situations, he was in despair. The plug had been pulled. Without the feeling that he was always staving off imminent disaster, he felt no drive to do his work. He realized that his usual high drive level made him feel powerful and able to take care of the complex demands of his business. Without it, he feared he would never be able to function well again. He said to me, genuinely frightened, "I guess I don't have any basic motivation at all." Yet he admitted that all aspects of the business seemed to be going well. It was his perception that he was doing nothing that was causing his discomfort. I encouraged him to keep going, to keep performing the three practices that enabled him to focus his attention on the here and now, pulling his mind back from the abyss of anxiety. He agreed.

■ RICHARD

Richard was pretty stressed out by his new job responsibility, but he already had some useful attention skills going for him. His atypical background as a commune child of hippie parents endowed him with better-than-average people skills, and he had formed an unusual perspective on his own role in the business world. Richard believed that his value as a human being was based on the degree to which he could ease the suffering of the people around him and the world in general. This expansive view was clearly helpful to him in managing his own stress level. Whenever he found himself getting upset over events at work that were out of his control, he shifted to a wider perspective in his mind and reminded himself that his real value to others lay in his humanity. He clearly had some inherent facility with *Skill 1: The Ability to Narrow or Widen the Mind's Focus at Will.* What made this skill important to managing his stress level was that he had a sense of his basic purpose regardless of what he was doing at any particular moment. This skill also enabled him to assign priorities easily. He had no trouble integrating new projects into an already scheduled day. What he needed to add to his repertoire was a finely tuned ability to sink into each task at hand, then leave it and sink into another one just as completely. He needed to become proficient at *Skill 2: The Mental Flexibility to Shift the Mind's Focus At Will from One Thing to Another.*

Richard was fascinated by the practices introduced in the class on simultaneous inclusion. He had always considered himself a pretty flexible thinker, but here were the means to hone himself further. He began with the segment of *Practice 2: Meditation on Movement (Object of Focus: sensations of the body as a reliable refuge from the perceptions of busyness)* that specifically deals with the development of mental flexibility, namely, *Exercises 8–10.* These miraculous little neurological calisthenics arouse the nervous system and expand it when one attempts to coordinate the movements of different parts of the body simultaneously. It doesn't even matter if one is successful in the coordination; the nervous system is stimulated in any case and the flexibility is assured. Richard was also interested in doing *Practice 3: Walking Meditation with Different Objects of Focus*, which required that he shift his attention from one focus to another in succession. Though slightly embarrassed that these practices were not initially easy for him, Richard was intrigued by what appeared after a few weeks to be an increased ability to concentrate on projects, even when interrupted, and he was inspired to continue.

■ EMMY

Emmy's life *seemed* to be working for her, but only superficially. Yes, she had *Skill 2: The Mental Flexibility to Shift the Mind's Focus at Will from One Thing to Another* developed to an amazing degree, sinking deeply into activity after activity at work, multitasking like the pro she was, going from meeting to computer screen to phone call without so much as a sigh, then attending to her leisure hours with the same relentless absorption. But as well as being highly structured and proactive, she needed to cultivate another mode: the ability to be unstructured and open. After the accident victim incident, Emmy began to pay conscious attention to her growing discomfiture with her ironclad life. She needed to move from the particular to the general, from the specific activity to the overall picture, to stay in touch with her changing needs and maturation process. She may not always want to live as she lives now, but as her determination to succeed brings her into more and more rarified financial environments, she has to keep asking herself: "Is this what I want? Is what I'm giving up worth what I'm getting?" This way, she keeps tabs on her changing ideals and lifestyle as she moves up in her chosen profession.

With her meditation background, Emmy was already aware of the power of full attention to alter one's perceptions of reality. A whiz at *Skill 2*, she promised to be a quick study for *Skill 1: The Ability to Narrow or Widen the Mind's Focus at Will.* To that end, she began doing *Practice 1: Wandering Mind Meditation: Sitting Still and Counting the Breath from 1–10 (Object of Focus: the various excursions our mind takes away from counting the breaths)*, with the added emphasis of specifically noticing the places where her mind wandered while she was counting her breaths and taking note of them, rather than instantly cutting them off. In other words, she lingered long enough to perceive and identify the thoughts that entered her counting before returning single-mindedly to it. Most of us don't have the problem in meditation that Emmy did; we struggle to return to our counting and don't consider it an effort to linger in our distracting thoughts. Emmy, on the other hand, needed to get broader in her focus, to have a wider perspective, to include more of her own randomness.

CHAPTER FIVE

Living Seamlessly

THE FLOW OF ACTIVITY

We need not view our work and leisure worlds as fundamentally different. If we train our minds to see our myriad tasks backlit by the inherent unity of them all, we can just live our lives, whether engaged in so-called work or leisure activity, completely aware of all the sensual, sensory, intellectual and purposeful aspects of all of our endeavors. When we highlight each activity with our full attention, we are continually connected to our own feelings, thoughts, sensations of our body and rhythm of the earth. The experience of our doing becomes much more dimensional than merely checking a task off our list at its completion.

What usually distracts us from multidimensional connections to each task is our preoccupation with the goal, the "why" of our activity. If we can soften the exclusively goal-specific focus that we usually bring to our work concerns and start to pay attention not just to what furthers our goals but to everything inside us and around us, we have vastly enlarged our own playing field. Our perspective on life radically changes when being aware is one of our concerns. Our daily preoccupations part to reveal our basic awareness, an aspect of consciousness that is always present if we train ourselves to notice it. When we pay close attention, we can see quite clearly the process by which we construct layers of concerns and worries that obscure this subtle wakefulness.

Awareness of this deep source of energy and peace allows us to see our lives as a simple flow of activity, not necessarily broken up into separate pursuits and tasks. When we're aware not only of having a goal and an end time for our work but also of our sensations, our perceptions, our physical motions, and our judgments in doing the work, there is a flexible, flowing feeling to our day. Rather than experiencing our work as a series of annoying transitions from this place to that and from this task to that, of starting and stopping and being interrupted again and again, our days begin to have a seamless quality because we are focused on action itself and all its sensual/perceptual/intellectual aspects. Our various faculties and talents surface as they are useful to us. Our assorted chores and projects are not valued in terms of how boring or urgent or empowering they are, but each gets our full attention in turn. When we wake up in the morning, we dip our hands into a river of activity and responsibility. When we stop for the evening, we lift our hands out of the river and let them rest. It's *all* the river, flowing toward the sunset, and it will deliver us into our bed.

If you abide exclusively in the workaday world and have no familiarity with nondual awareness, your entire life is goal-oriented, a series of unending chores and demands. On the other hand, if you vastly prefer to hang out in nondual aware-ness, reveling in sensation and avoiding the everyday world of distinct values, you won't be able to take care of your life. But if you succeed in simultaneously including both states of mind, whether you are slaving away or lying on the beach, you will be able to perceive your different activities as simply breaking up the nondual into names and concepts that you will manipulate in order to get things done. This is the same process you used as you left the world of color and form in *Practice 3, number 5* to return to "trees" and "chairs." And as you sit at your desk and prioritize your workday tasks according to their relative urgency, you understand that none of these tasks has any greater or lesser inherent value. You yourself assign them value according to the circumstances of the moment. Basically, you're just living your life, dipping in and out of the activity river, so confident in your ability to follow your course, to get more or less calm or frenetic as you wish, that you dare to challenge yourself by getting out of your well-regulated current and plunging into a raging torrent from time to time. This is called "willingly giving yourself up to the anxiety and confusion of a particular situation." The gist of it is that you go into a frenzied office place with hysterical coworkers and offer yourself up to their chaos, allowing your state of mind to be infected with their dis-ease. The only difference between you and them is that you're doing it consciously and voluntarily. How different this feels from being forcibly tied to a roller coaster and jerked around the track.

WHY WE CLING TO BUSYNESS

It Protects Us from Emptiness

Up there with our favorite drugs and distractions from facing the terror of loneliness and existential emptiness is our current national pastime, "busyness." People brag to each other about how busy they are, with the clear implication that they are valued and indispensable to the unending projects that fill their waking hours. But should a little slit appear in the cloth of their densely woven consciousness, allowing an open space to appear, then there's a stab of panic. If the slit is not immediately repaired, filled up with thoughts and opinions, it threatens to become a gaping hole through which we would see—we know not what! But the menace of self-annihilation is definitely nearby. Few of us stay with this image long enough to feel the panic fully; most of us veer off to the next thing. But, in fact, those of us who suspect that this encounter with *nothingness* heralds the obliteration of our personal self by existential emptiness (the absence of thought or purpose) are right. That's exactly what happens. It's just that the actual experience of losing track of one's self is not what it looks like before it actually happens. It's kind of like jumping out of an airplane. The thought of it is terrifying, but people who parachute-jump for pleasure describe the tremendous exhilaration they experience after making the leap. They let go of the fear of jumping while they're in the doorway of the plane. A split second later, they are grinning broadly, tumbling in a free fall of ecstatic enjoyment. Similarly, the first scary glimpse of nothingness is not at all indicative of what lies hidden in the unoccupied mind. Cut loose from premeditated thoughts, the mind will settle at its own relatively peaceful level, just like the mud in a pond settles and the water clears after the kids have ended their swim.

Meditators know this well and look forward to their regular periods of experiencing a relatively quiet mind contemplating a pleasant parade of bits of old songs, snatches of long-ago conversation, the sounds of children playing outside the meditation-room window, the punch line from some comedian's joke. Meditators know well that the idea of "self" eventually disappears to be replaced by the infinite space of basic awareness, a realm where the limiting notions of "I" and "my" are flotsam and jetsam floating on the boundless ocean of being.

Most of us don't specifically intend to use busyness as a defense against the existential pain of existence. In fact, we are very much aware that our preoccupation with a demanding workload is costing us the opportunity to explore other realms. We have long been cognizant of other selves inside us, clamoring to be expressed. We'd love to take art classes, singing lessons, skiing instruction. We'd love to be a better parent and devote more time to our children's interests. Yet we never put aside the time. In fact, when we stay home with a cold longer than a day—the first day is easy, we just sleep and watch daytime TV—we get some taste of what an unstructured, undemanding life might be like. And we say to ourselves that it's not as desirable as it seems when we imagine lying on the beach somewhere while we're still in front of the computer at midnight. If we spend years full of nonstop activity, and we pause, inadvertently allowing an empty space to arise—bare consciousness without a direction or a purpose—the first glimpse of *nothingness* can be pretty daunting. It's like looking over a cliff and not being able to see the bottom of a chasm: Alice tumbling down the White Rabbit's hole! Rushing stark-staring insane into the Existential Void! Certain annihilation.

But if we're too busy to notice the sky reflected in a dewdrop or too harried to turn to answer a child's call, the neurological blip that brings on the instantaneous disappearance and reestablishment of the logic and purpose of our life could be scary indeed. However, the sudden apprehension of the ultimate meaninglessness of our life is only upsetting if our life is precariously balanced on a shaky foundation of the completion of chores and goal-oriented projects. If we have constructed a life around our own deepest needs and the expression of our natures, an unexpected collision with that black hole in our consciousness doesn't undo us. We're already home. Meaningless as our own individual life might be in the ultimate scheme of things, that knowledge doesn't make our pursuits any less interesting. The activities we do, the people we care for—they are enough.

It Makes Us Feel Alive

Some of us love the frenetic glamour of the "roller coaster ride" produced by a certain working style: meeting a series of urgent deadlines, running on speed and caffeine through the wee smalls, rising a few hours later to present the resulting project to an important client, then crashing right after the meeting to sleep for a few days. We are wound tightly as a coil for days and weeks, then catch a plane to the tropics for a complete meltdown as soon as the project is over. There's a lot to recommend this mode of work/rest in terms of its drama, its edginess. It confirms the fact that we are indeed alive, since we might have some doubts. Up through our numbness surges the adrenaline rush of fear and then the soaring relief of triumph. We can feel that aliveness pulsing through our body: The client loved it! The deadline is met! The fee is collected! Yes, we are alive! We know it now! And most importantly, the intensity distracts us from the slowly dawning suspicion that our life means nothing, that all our efforts have not brought us any closer to happiness.

It Shields Us from the Suffering Around Us

Despite the poignant inadequacy of merely getting things done as a way to feel alive, keeping busy does do one very useful thing for us: it keeps us from actually feeling the pain resulting from the overwhelming suffering we see and feel around us every day. If we live in a city or even a small town, we come into contact daily with the suffering of homeless people. If we tune in to the nightly news or pick up a newspaper, we learn of people overwhelmed by grief because they've lost their child, their friend, their health. If the majority of our consciousness is taken up by checking off yet another chore on our checklist, we stay on an emotional even keel. As taskdoers, worker bees, we hit one note and play it over and over again. We bury ourselves in activity the way substance abusers bury themselves in drink or drugs; no matter how many things we race to do during the day, there's always something more to be done. When there is a threat of hurt or disappointment due to circumstances beyond our control, there's no time to feel it. The monthly sales figures have to be calculated, the client gifts selected and sent, the copier contract gone over, the boardroom reserved for a partners meeting. The substance abuser's overall feeling is unpleasant enough—frantic, uneasy—but he does manage to avoid the real lows: the grief, the anger, the disillusionment.

Our coworker tells us she's getting a divorce. We offer support, knowing our efforts to comfort and reassure her are pallid in view of the amount of consolation that's actually needed: the gestures of support and hours of consolation that would take so much time—way too much time. We climb on a bus and see an old woman struggling with her parcels. Involuntarily the thought crosses our mind: that may be me someday. This is an image too painful to bear. Passing a street corner, an adolescent boy, dirty and grim-faced, panhandles us for money. He might be a runaway from what we don't even want to suppose. An abusive father? A sexually aggressive stepfather? A negligent mother addicted to crack? We tell ourselves, don't even go there. It's too wrenching to imagine the life he ran away from.

We visit our mother in the Midwest and notice she's getting a little forgetful. Her doctor tells us he's concerned that she hasn't paid her bill in several months. We push away from our minds this first dawning of her inevitable dependence.

We're sitting in a playground and across the way we see a mother slap her toddler. The child howls its startled objection. Outraged, we rise from our bench to protest; then as mother continues her conversation and child, wiping his tears, turns back to play, we realize it's over before we even get there. There's nothing to be done but absorb the blow quietly, just like the child has learned to do. What's ahead for this mother and child we don't want to dwell upon.

Our supervisor makes a lunch date and after the chicken salad is served, she tells us she has just been diagnosed with breast cancer and wants to know how much responsibility we'd be ready to assume during her medical leave. We feel helpless, staggeringly inadequate to deal with this upcoming loss and grief.

All these vignettes are about mundane anguish, the daily suffering that we see and are inescapably involved with, whether we want to be or not. It's unutterably sad and painful, but its frequency makes it mundane. In order to avoid it, we'd have to live in a cave. In the short term, busyness as a strategy to keep ourselves insulated from feeling our mundane anguish can be very useful. It can get us through uneasy waiting periods like the few days before the doctor calls us with the results of our biopsy. It can keep us active after a catastrophe like a fire in our home. It can keep us interactive after our child is hurt in an accident. So the one-note pitch of busyness can be useful in the short term.

But if busyness is used habitually as a long-term strategy to deal with the ups and downs of everyday life, eventually it robs us of our interest and vitality. To stay busy and functional, no matter what happens in the world or in our personal lives, it is necessary that we cut off all feeling and sensation arising from our bodies and our emotions. As we get busier and busier, allotting more and more of our hours and days to a schedule, eventually our world is extremely ordered and controlled. We come to live in some tiny little strip of consciousness, maybe just what is needed to get up, go to work, come home, and park ourselves in front of the TV or go to yet another civic meeting. We can't afford to have any experiences that would throw the whole thing off, like stopping to help a stranded motorist or giving some real attention to the stray thought that our teenage son might be spending too much time alone in his room. It would be counterproductive to allow spontaneous feeling to break through our busyness or come to rest in the physicality of our bodies, exciting our feelings. We might get derailed. But if we persist in shutting out any trace of our pain or fear, we eventually live on narrow, bleak little tundras of our own creation. Is this a life worth living?

CHAPTER SIX

The Ones Who Are Not Busy

From focusing on her body using the Body Awareness exercises of *Practice 2: Meditation on Movement, Exercises 1–6: Body Awareness* Nancy learned to shift her focus of attention from her ideal of perfection, which is always there in her mind, to the actual physical and sensory components of her work activity as she moved about her office. She also enjoyed her daily excursion into raw perception through *Practice 3: Walking Meditation with Different Objects of Focus* on her beach walk and thought it was the most helpful practice she did in terms of subverting her habit of conceptualizing her whole life. As she walked along the beach, she could now value her sense impressions as they came to her rather than walking blindly and thinking about work.

Consciousness of her bodily and sense impressions enabled her to develop an engrossing focal point to counter the weight of her perfection addiction. Aware of her kinesthetic reality, she was able to notice the yearning of her body to exercise and the longing of her intellect to leave the convoluted details of her casework and focus on something relaxing, like the blue sky or her husband's face. She was delighted with her achievement. Thus, she settled happily into a full life at last, infusing her work with sensory awareness and opening her heart to all that her life included.

■ LUANN

The real surprise for LuAnn was not only that the movement training seemed to center her deeply and clear her mind for the next project at work, but also that she seemed to be making less of an emotional distinction between work and home. She gave up her lifelong habit of putting work first, and instead prioritized ALL her tasks in the morning for that day, mixing work and home chores together. Thus, she was free to focus her full attention on each task at the time she was doing every one. The result was a much more fulfilling and less stressful way of keeping up with everything she had to do. She was relaxed and present in every situation, whether laying out a page or making soup.

■ KEN

When we left Ken, he was attempting to integrate his emotional responses into his product evaluation sessions at work, an advanced simultaneous-inclusion skill since it involved focusing on his feelings and communicating with others at the same time. He had started by sequentially focusing on the meeting, then his emotions, then the meeting, then his emotions. But gradually he was able to simultaneously include his emotional feeling while he was concentrating on the comments of his superiors at the meeting. At that point the comments made during these meetings informed his body—it generated emotion—but his emotion began to inform his participation in the meetings as well, and his body was released from its solitary role of registering emotion. When he finally was able to tune in to what his body absorbed every day, he was astonished at the intensity of the emotional roller coaster that he boarded each morning at work and rode all day long. In order to do his job, he had become numb to his stress level.

Ken was truly amazed when he found out how much information there was in this practice that had eluded him before. He was equally impressed with how useful it was to know how he felt in various situations. He would never have guessed how fearful he was of criticism, nor how personally invested he was in others' approval of his ideas. Similarly, including his own feelings in his discussions with his girlfriend made it much easier to inspire her understanding when he was too tired to go out. Ironically, however, he actually had much more energy, now that the energy tied up in numbing himself was available to him. Newly aware of what his job was costing him in terms of emotional stress and physical strain, Ken decided to work part-time, at least until his headaches and muscle spasms subsided. The bonus was that he now had plenty of energy for other activities. He went hiking with his girlfriend, which she loved, and took up bicycling with other friends. He has no regrets.

■ MICHAEL

When I ran into Michael a week after he had been seized with terror at the prospect that he did not possess any inherent motivation to make things go well at work, he was a different person. The ability to focus on each task sequentially rather than creating panic by focusing on everything all at once, freed him from his fantasies of ultimate ruin and eventually enabled him to sense something a little more subtle: his own natural energy and inclination. He could feel his own real engine beginning to chug. He had gotten in touch with the yearnings of his own creativity. Thrilled with this delightful turn of events, he was back to thinking about nightlife activities.

■ RICHARD

Using the segment of *Practice 2: Meditation on Movement (Object of Focus: sensations of the body as a reliable refuge from the perception of busyness)* that specifically dealt with the development of mental flexibility, and *Practice 3: Walking Meditation with Different Objects of Focus,* Richard had not only become a multitasker par excellence, loving the challenge of adding more and more projects to juggle, but he was able to sink deeply into each one, bringing with his focus the attention to detail and care with which Richard was uniquely endowed. He could spend ten or twenty single-minded minutes on a project, then attend to an interruption with the same unwavering focus the previous project had received. What his simultaneous inclusion practices had taught him rendered him one of the most valuable employees in his national company. He began to enjoy the perks that solvent companies bestow on employees they are grooming for corporate responsibility.

Richard had such success learning mental agility to better manage his work stress that he even liked to practice it just for fun. He began running, a sport that had always appealed to him.

His ability to focus on different aspects of his physical and mental exertion while running made him a marathon participant in less than a year.

■ EMMY

Counting her breaths as she'd learned to in *Practice 1*, with the emphasis on lingering briefly at the places her mind wandered to rather than immediately cutting them off, eventually enabled Emmy to incorporate her developing values into her work activity. She is climbing steadily in her profession and grounds herself at every level. As her network of contacts expands, she has been able to choose specific working environments based on the values of her coworkers and her keen aesthetic sensibility. She wishes to surround herself with like-minded people and beauty, and she has done so.

In each case, awareness of their moment-to-moment direct experience helped each of these people to examine the congruence of their daily events with their most important values. This kind of alignment, sustained by focusing full attention on our actual experience, is crucial to making the choices in our lives that will make us truly happy. If our choices are limited by our circumstances—if we have no alternative but to work at a job we hate in order to support children who came along unexpectedly—then we need to direct our full attention toward noticing the relief that grows between the cracks of our oppression: the pleasure of praise, a joke shared with coworkers inducing momentary muscle relaxation, the sudden smile of a pleased customer. If we cultivate the mental flexibility to protect our consciousness from settling into a rigid glower, then moment-to-moment awareness will allow the light to shine into our cell.

The Commentary for the 21st Case (page 32) also notes that while Daowu asserted the existence of only one moon—one reality—for the sake of his debate with Yunyan, he knew very well that "on the other hand, there is not only a second moon— a second point of view—there are infinite moons, myriad moons, a moon for every point of view, every person, in the world."[4] We all view our world differently according to our beliefs, our emotional states, and where we're standing. This flexibility holds enormous potential for us to view our circumstances in ways that benefit our lives and drastically reduce unwanted stress. We need not be stuck in one view forever.

CHAPTER SEVEN

A Question of Values

THE DISTRACTION OF DESIRE

There's a dawning consciousness among mainstream American workers that the strenuous efforts of the past few decades or so to get really wealthy, to "have it all," to work oneself into oblivious pulp for a few years then retire young, haven't really worked out. Whether you're one of those who went bust in the dot-com crash or whose ambitious dreams were dashed with the resultant scarcity of high-end jobs, whether the end of your joyride was intentional or involuntary, you might have already suspected that devotion of your time and energy to the satisfaction of a series of momentary desires not arising from your deepest yearnings was beginning to pall.

For some time in our culture, it's been all about material things. People talk openly about how much they paid for their houses and their tchotchkes, taboo topics in polite society a few decades ago. In some high schools, even a teenager's prowess at sports is trumped by the ownership of prestigious items in the popularity contest that dominates adolescent consciousness. With consumer confidence as the basis of Western economic health, we are barraged with constant messages encouraging us to accumulate ever-more stuff, to buy bigger houses in which to put the stuff, and to consider this amassing of serious stuff in compliance with the unalienable right of the "pursuit of happiness" set out in the Declaration of Independence.

But is the agreeable blip of acquisition really an adequate paradigm for happiness? We're conditioned to crave things, to work hard to accumulate them, to enjoy them, and then to continue to work hard to get something new with its promise of a fresh kind of enjoyment. The implication is that the manipulation of sequentially novel possessions is enough to build a lifestyle around.

Deeper values like friendship, loyalty, accomplishment, service and integrity get short shrift in a culture built on acquisition because several of these values conflict with the behaviors most conducive to the efficient accumulation of material goods. People who derive satisfaction from creating a well-run business don't usually falsify their company's profits in order to cash out their shares at a high price before bailing on the company altogether. People who value service to others probably weren't among those persons who filed applications for nonexistent relatives in order to collect some of the money donated to the Red Cross after the events of September 11, 2001. However, the experience of living a life based on the assumptions of interdependence and mutual support may be a much more satisfying way to live than that based on the perception of scarcity and fear that dominate a worldview in which acquisition and competition are primary.

We've all been conditioned since childhood to focus on getting things as an indication of achievement, be it material like a new car, or intangible like a promotion. We experience this striving in endless subtle forms all the time. We cook our food in order to have dinner. We wash our clothes in order to have clean clothes. We go to work to make money in order to eat, to have shelter, to buy things we desire. We get on the bus in order to go someplace, and so on. Much of our activity is to produce a desired result. This makes a lot of sense. It's common sense. The trouble with thinking this way, though, is that it tends to focus us on the outcome rather than on the effort of our activity itself. We barely notice the cooking, the cleaning, the bus ride, the working, except that it takes time away from what we think we *really* want to do. And after so many years of looking ahead to the results of our doing rather than focusing on the doing itself, we don't even notice the taste of the food, the smell of the clean clothes, the moment we leap off the bus at our destination ("Wow! I'm here!"), the brief but hallowed moment of receiving our paycheck. We're trained now to focus ahead—to the next paycheck perhaps. This one's already spent and therefore no fun. We miss whatever's in front of us.

It may seem trivial to you which one you focus on: preparing the meal or eating the meal. Or neither one—you're off in some fantasy most of the time. But the accumulated effects of spending our time on earth always looking ahead create a kind of craving, a hungry-ghost mentality (the hungry ghost is a mythological creature with a huge belly and a tiny mouth; these anatomical features destine the hungry ghost to a bitter existence of forever craving without any satisfaction) that is always one step ahead, on to the next thing, never settling, never resting, never contented, never appreciating. This sets the scene for continual existential dissatisfaction. We're never here; we're always there. This is the difference between happiness and merely satisfying a desire. This is huge in terms of how able we are to satisfy our deepest yearnings. The training for happiness is in the little things, like washing clothes or riding the bus, but the proof of the pudding is in the big picture. Are you happy right now, reading this page? Or are you chasing the next big thing?

INTEGRATING OUR OVERALL VALUES

One path to the happiness we all seek is to cultivate the ability to throw ourselves into our activity without reservation, with our whole heart, holding back nothing, regardless of the likelihood of particular results. We become adept at totally immersing ourselves into what is before us, what is under our nose that needs to be done. When our mind wanders, we know how to bring it back into alignment with what our hands are actually doing and what our eyes are truly looking at. Since what is before one changes continually, we find our mental flexibility training helpful *(Practice 3* and *Practice 4)*. We can apply these same skills to resisting the distractions of greed, worry and projections onto the future.

The skills of focus we learned in the various coordination exercises we did while studying *Meditation on Movement,* in *Practice 2,* doing the *Walking Meditation with Different Objects of Focus* in *Practice 3,* and especially the *Talking Meditation* in *Practice 4* become very important when we look at our specific activities from the perspective of our values—our basic beliefs about what we think our lives should exemplify. Noticing that our values can inform our choice of activities is analogous to the nondual realm informing our world of things and the relative values we assign to those things. This is the simultaneous inclusion of the basic values that we hold dear and the details of our current activity. When we look at our everyday world activities from the point of view of our highest values, we examine those activities through the lens of our beliefs about what is important to us overall. If doing no harm to others is one of our highest standards for our own behavior, then our job as manager of the department of a large company should probably not require that we winnow the employees under us in accordance with some arbitrary corporate policy that overlooks their individual contribution.

After thirty years of rising through the ranks of a manufacturing company to become a department manager, Larry, an ardent humanist, was presented with that very dilemma following a bad year for the company. When he was forced by the new company policy to fire several employees whose performances were good, just not as good as the best performers in his department, Larry decided to retire several years earlier than planned. The interesting aspect of his situation from our focusing-attention point of view is that he spent over a year firing people (one a good friend) because he was focused on his obligation to his company and his immediate boss. Carrying out the firings proved to be so stressful for him that he shifted his focus to his actual feelings during the firing task. Though he had been aware of his feelings before when he was focused mainly on his obligations as a manager, he shifted his focus so that his feelings now came to the fore. He immediately concluded he could not do another firing and began to focus instead on a retirement strategy.

After we have learned to hold our deepest values constantly before us while being aware of the minutiae of our daily activities, we are ready to evaluate every act we do in terms of how we want to spend time, what we want to be accomplishing, how we want to be living, and what aspects of ourselves we want to strengthen or diminish. People's lives take on an added dimension of satisfaction when they begin to tailor their activities to reflect their deepest sensibilities. Being present to both our values and our immediate experience, we don't get bogged down in wondering whether this job is worth the money or whether we should either adjust to a less-than-perfect situation or leave altogether. The information is right there, in our feelings, in our body sensations, every moment of our workday. We may decide the money is worth the discomfort for a time, but it will never be a question of our not registering the discomfort involved. We won't waste time going over our deadline nor bemoaning our helplessness.

This takes resentment and victimization out of such decisions. You take full responsibility for your need to make the money at the expense of your pleasure. If you make the decision the other way, you take full responsibility for making less money because you choose to enjoy the activities of your job over the less-than-munificent financial compensation. This way of making decisions based on your actual experience of the activities involved is profoundly empowering, satisfying, grounding. You have the full information you need from your body and mind to call the shots.

CHAPTER EIGHT

Conclusion

EFFORT WITHOUT DESIRE

Because we have been educated to put so much importance on our ability to formulate thoughts and concepts, we tend to live our lives dominated by personal opinion. It's actually much easier to live this way. It takes less effort to have a simple reactive response to something rather than to attend to our inevitably complex, confusing immediate experience. We can sleepwalk through our lives if we want to do that. The heavy downside of accepting our unthinking opinions about things, however, is that they lock us into fixed ideas that limit what we are able to do or say. They limit our liveliness, our enjoyment of our encounters, and our activities. Worse, the possibility of some new behavior gets less and less the more we rely on our habitual reactions. Preconceptions are how we separate ourselves from actual experience and thereby how we make our lives monotonous and insensible.

We slip out from under our preconceptions when we become absorbed in our immediate activity. Putting aside our huge warehouse of opinions is the act of just doing a task with awareness of the body sensations involved in the task, the swinging door of breath-in, breath-out, the thoughts necessary to organize and project the next steps in the task, the sense impressions of our immediate environment. The great thirteenth-century Zen master Dogen said, "Realization . . . is effort without desire."[5] When we understand that we are happiest giving everything our full attention—without concern for the outcome—we have had a great insight into the nature of the human heart.

This also points out the importance of creativity in our lives. "Effort without desire" refers to the attitude of an artist creating a painting or sculpture, a poet carefully picking the words that express her feeling, a scientist recording his data, a mother making cookies. The activities that express our creative impulses are the most deeply satisfying activities we can do, but we can also bring this attitude to the activities that we find less than engrossing and imbue them with the same importance that makes our poems and paintings so precious. We can commit our whole selves to them for the time that we spend doing them. We can do the dishes, living through each plate and cup that we scrub with soapy water and make clean; we can fix the faucet with total attention to the wrench and pipe; we can drive home with total awareness of our tired bodies, the other cars around us, the vibes on the highway (ever notice how drivers on the same street or highway are mostly all in the same mood?), the music on the CD player; we can have a conversation with a stranger asking directions on the street with the same attention and consideration we would bring to an exchange with a close friend.[6]

With this attitude, any work or job we do is meaningful. We are our activity itself, cultivating the doing of work for its own sake, totally immersed in the feelings and sensations of physical movement, creative thought, supporting the flow of life. By giving our daily movements our full attention, our mind has a chance to unfold, revealing psychic space around pain in which we can find relief, not because the pain has stopped but because we are able to focus on the gap between the pulsations of pain, the space around mundane chores, the space around everything. This kind of space is always there in our psyches, available to receive us. The One Who Is Not Busy is always there, aware of our muscles working, aware of the breeze on our cheeks.

To give every activity, every person, every phone call our

wholehearted attention poses a radical shift in our self-reward system. Instead of considering the finished product of our effort the whole point of doing an activity, we view the activity itself—the muscle movements, the sensory accompaniment, the creative ideation, the sense of movement and space—as an end in itself.

When we are able to sink beneath our ideas and opinions into the immediacy of our actual experience, there is nothing further to look for—no directions, no reasons and no expectations. At the moment when we are exactly here, doing each thing for its own sake, being present right now, right here, we give our activity our whole heart and being. This is our greatest challenge and the deepest satisfaction in our lives.

1. Mihaly Csikszentmihalyi, *Flow: The Psychology of Optimal Experience* (St. Helens, Oregon: Perennial, 1993), 23.

2. Wayne Muller, *Sabbath: Finding Rest, Renewal, and Delight in Our Busy Lives* (Boston: Bantam Books, 2000), 70.

3. Darlene Cohen, *Turning Suffering Inside Out* (Berkeley: Shambhala, 2002), 202.

4. Thomas Cleary, trans., *Book of Serenity* (Berkeley: Shambhala, 1998), 91–95.

5. Kazuaki Tanahashi, ed., *Moon in a Dewdrop: Writings of Zen Master Dogen* (New York: North Point Press, 1995), 218–19.

6. Darlene Cohen, *Turning Suffering Inside Out* (Berkeley: Shambhala, 2000), 220–21.